EXAMINING ON-GOING CHALLENGES AT THE U.S. SECRET SERVICE AND THEIR GOVERNMENT-WIDE IMPLICATIONS

JOINT HEARING

BEFORE THE

SUBCOMMITTEE ON OVERSIGHT
AND MANAGEMENT EFFICIENCY

OF THE

COMMITTEE ON HOMELAND SECURITY

HOUSE OF REPRESENTATIVES

AND THE

SUBCOMMITTEE ON REGULATORY AFFAIRS
AND FEDERAL MANAGEMENT

OF THE

COMMITTEE ON HOMELAND SECURITY

AND GOVERNMENTAL AFFAIRS

UNITED STATES SENATE

ONE HUNDRED FOURTEENTH CONGRESS

FIRST SESSION

NOVEMBER 17, 2015

Serial No. 114–43

Printed for the use of the Committee on Homeland Security

Available via the World Wide Web: http://www.gpo.gov/fdsys/

U.S. GOVERNMENT PUBLISHING OFFICE

99–749 PDF   WASHINGTON : 2016

For sale by the Superintendent of Documents, U.S. Government Publishing Office
Internet: bookstore.gpo.gov   Phone: toll free (866) 512–1800; DC area (202) 512–1800
Fax: (202) 512–2104   Mail: Stop IDCC, Washington, DC 20402–0001

(II)

CONTENTS

VI

EXAMINING ON-GOING CHALLENGES AT THE U.S. SECRET SERVICE AND THEIR GOVERNMENT-WIDE IMPLICATIONS

Tuesday, November 17, 2015

U.S. House of Representatives,
Committee on Homeland Security,
Subcommittee on Oversight and Management
Efficiency, and
U.S. Senate,
Committee on Homeland Security and
Governmental Affairs,
Subcommittee on Regulatory Affairs and
Federal Management,
Washington, DC.

The subcommittees met, pursuant to call, at 10:01 a.m., in Room 210, HVC, Hon. Scott Perry [Chairman of the House Committee on Homeland Security, Subcommittee on Oversight and Management Efficiency] presiding.

Present from the Subcommittee on Oversight and Management Efficiency: Representatives Perry, Watson Coleman, Thompson, Duncan, Clawson, Torres, Carter, and Loudermilk.

Present from the Subcommittee on Regulatory Affairs and Federal Management: Senators Lankford, Heitkamp, Johnson, and Peters.

Mr. PERRY. The House Committee on Homeland Security, Subcommittee on Oversight and Management Efficiency and the Senate Committee on Homeland Security and Governmental Affairs, Subcommittee on Regulatory Affairs and Federal Management will come to order.

The purpose of this hearing is to examine failures at the U.S. Secret Service and their implications Government-wide.

The Chair recognizes himself for an opening statement.

In September, the DHS Office of Inspector General, the OIG, released a report on its 4-month-long investigation into improper access and distribution of information within the Secret Service. The findings were alarming.

Wide-spread violations of the Privacy Act and an agency policy occurred by Secret Service employees who accessed and distributed information on a Member of Congress' past employment application and senior management did nothing immediately to stop it.

Inspector General John Roth stated that the episode was deeply disturbing. In addition, Director Clancy announced he had a different account of what he initially told OIG. Investigators subsequently had to re-interview Director Clancy and issue an addendum to the report.

This incident leaves numerous questions unanswered. How did this happen? Why did Secret Service leadership not act and why and how did Director Clancy change his account almost immediately after the IG's report was released? The American people deserve answers. DHS must hold all employees involved appropriately accountable.

As disturbing as this incident is, it is only one example of other instances where Secret Service employees showed very poor judgment and leadership failed to act.

Earlier this year, senior agents who may have been under the influence of alcohol compromised an area at the White House being investigated for a suspicious package. Director Clancy was, again, not immediately informed.

Late last year, OIG also reported about a 2011 incident where agents were diverted to investigate an accident at the home of—correction—an incident at the home of the director's assistant, which appeared to be a misuse of agency resources and violation of the Federal Employee Code of Ethics.

The findings in the IG's latest report are yet another example of damage to the American people's trust in the Secret Service. When scandal after scandal emerges and the management is ill-informed or fails to act, the American people have cause for great concern. We entrust the Secret Service with tremendous authorities and tools. When they abuse those authorities, they violate their contract with the American people.

Because of the Service's recent failures, DHS Secretary Jeh Johnson convened a panel of experts late last year to recommend changes to improve the service. The panel made broad recommendations in December 2014 related to training and personnel, perimeter security, technology and operation, and leadership. The panel's report provided a broad road map to begin reforming the service. I expect Director Clancy to fully explain today what progress has been made in implementing the panel's recommendations.

While Congress has a responsibility to conduct rigorous oversight of the latest incident, we must also understand what is being done to improve the overall management of the Secret Service.

I am also concerned that similar abuses and shortcomings could occur in other Federal law enforcement agencies. It is important to understand what policies and safeguards, if any, are in place to prevent similar abuse regardless of whether it is as a Member of Congress or one of our constituents back home. If it happened at the Service, what is to say other Federal agencies are any better?

Today's hearing must be about more than pointing fingers. The American people have high expectations, as they should, for the Secret Service and want the agency to be successful. Their mission is absolutely critical to our Nation's well-being and, as we saw from excellent work by Secret Service personnel during the papal visit, and United States—correction—United Nations General Assembly, the Service can succeed with proper focus and leadership.

I look forward to hearing more from our witnesses on how the Secret Service can best overcome recent obstacles to improve the management and reform the culture of this critical agency.

[The statement of Chairman Perry follows:]

STATEMENT OF CHAIRMAN SCOTT PERRY

NOVEMBER 17, 2015

In September, the DHS Office of Inspector General (OIG) released a report on its 4-month-long investigation into improper access and distribution of information within the Secret Service. The findings were alarming: Wide-spread violations of the Privacy Act and agency policy occurred by Secret Service employees who accessed and distributed information on a Member of Congress's past employment application and senior management did nothing immediately to stop it. Inspector General John Roth stated that the episode was "deeply disturbing." In addition, Director Clancy announced he had a different account of what he initially told OIG. Investigators subsequently had to reinterview Director Clancy and issue an addendum to the report.

This incident leaves numerous questions unanswered: How did this happen, why did Secret Service leadership not act, and why and how did Director Clancy change his account almost immediately after the IG's report is released? The American people deserve answers. DHS must hold all employees involved appropriately accountable. As disturbing as this incident is, it is only one example of other instances where Secret Service employees showed very poor judgment and leadership failed to act. Earlier this year, senior agents who may have been under the influence of alcohol, compromised an area at the White House being investigated for a suspicious package. Director Clancy was again not immediately informed. Late last year, OIG also reported about a 2011 incident where agents were diverted to investigate an incident at the home of the director's assistant, which appeared to be a misuse of agency resources and violation of the Federal employee Code of Ethics.

The findings in the IG's latest report are yet another example of damage to the American people's trust in the Secret Service. When scandal after scandal emerges and management is ill-informed or fails to act, the American people have cause for great concern. We entrust the Secret Service with tremendous authorities and tools. When they abuse those authorities, they violate their contract with the American people.

Because of the Service's recent failures, DHS Secretary Jeh Johnson convened a panel of experts late last year to recommend changes to improve the Service. The panel made broad recommendations in December 2014 related to training and personnel; perimeter security, technology, and operations; and leadership. The panel's report provided a broad road map to begin reforming the Service. I expect Director Clancy to fully explain today what progress has been made in implementing the panel's recommendations. While Congress has a responsibility to conduct rigorous oversight of the latest incident, we must also understand what is being done to improve the overall management of the Secret Service.

I am also concerned that similar abuses and shortcomings could occur in other Federal law enforcement agencies. It's important to understand what policies and safeguards, if any, are in place to prevent similar abuse regardless of whether it's a Member of Congress or one of our constituents back home. If it happened at the Service, what's to say other Federal agencies are any better?

Today's hearing must be about more than pointing fingers. The American people have high expectations for the Secret Service and want the agency to be successful. Their mission is absolutely critical to our Nation's well-being and as we saw from the excellent work by Secret Service personnel during the papal visit and United Nations General Assembly, the Service can succeed with the proper focus and leadership. I look forward to hearing more from our witnesses on how the Secret Service can best overcome recent obstacles to improve the management and reform the culture of this critical agency.

Mr. PERRY. The Chair now recognizes the Chairman of the Senate Committee on Homeland Security and Governmental Affairs, Subcommittee on Regulatory Affairs and Federal Management, the gentleman from Oklahoma, Mr. Lankford, for his statement.

Senator LANKFORD. Chairman Perry, thank you very much. Thanks for holding this joint hearing with our subcommittee, as well.

Good morning, everyone. I am trying to think of a more awkward situation than how we are currently seated here but I am sure there is a way through a separate room; we are so far away from each other on this panel setting. I do appreciate everyone here. Hopefully this will be an open dialogue as we walk through this process together.

I do hope this also sheds some important light on the situation where we are at, not only with the Secret Service but Government-wide. At the outset, I would like to acknowledge the essential role that Secret Service fills and its incredible dedication to our country. We do appreciate very much the service the Secret Service brings to our Nation and what it has done historically and what it continues to do.

However, recent history of high-profile and embarrassing scandals of the Secret Service and the latest DHS inspector general findings of wrongdoing can't be swept under the rug, as I know Secret Service is not doing.

IG's investigation revealed unauthorized database searches of protected information began during a House Oversight and Government Reform hearing in March of this year. In the days that followed, many in the Secret Service continued to misuse their authority to access the sensitive employment history of Chairman Jason Chaffetz.

The IG's report noted that 60 instances of unauthorized access to the database by 45 Secret Service employees had violated the Privacy Act—excuse me—as well as an internal and DHS policies. The report also noted that 18 senior Secret Service executives failed to stop the unauthorized access or to inform Director Clancy about the unauthorized accesses.

In fairness, the report does reflect that one special agent instructed her subordinates to cease accessing the database. On its face, such wide-spread violations of our law and the public's trust are deeply disturbing. The IG did not question those involved if this was the only time they have inappropriately used the database.

In the internet age, everyone is concerned about the possibility that personal information could be stolen or misused. Our elite law enforcement agencies are not above the law and those responsible must face appropriate consequences. But, to me, there is a much bigger issue.

In these days, millions of Americans' personal data is stored across many Government agencies. The GAO report released earlier this year on the Government's Federal information security showed alarming findings. From 2009 to 2014, the number of information security incidents involving personally-identifiable information reported by Federal agencies has more than doubled.

GAO has stated that many agencies have largely failed to fully implement the hundreds of recommendations previously made to remedy security control vulnerabilities.

These security weaknesses continue to exist and the protection of significant personal data of millions of Americans housed by the IRS, HHS, the VA, and other agencies.

Just this month, the Social Security Administration's Office of the Inspector General released a report showing that the Social Security Administration paid monetary awards to 50 employees who were previously discovered to have accessed personal information of others without authorization.

Fifty Federal employees who accessed the personal information of others without authorization, yet, incredibly, in the end, they were rewarded despite breaking the law.

In another troublesome example the Senate Homeland Security Committee received testimony this year that a whistleblower was retaliated against for shedding light on inadequate suicide prevention practices at a V.A. hospital. This whistleblower learned that V.A. employees illegally and improperly accessed his private medical records after he brought to light the shameful behavior occurring at the V.A. hospital where he serves.

The question is now how do we fix this problem so that Americans believe that Government will protect their information and not use it for nefarious means? I am hopeful today we can take a step forward to address this issue, and would like to thank Director Clancy, Inspector General Roth, and Mr. Willemssen for their testimony today.

I look forward to examining these challenges with each of you.

[The statement of Chairman Lankford follows:]

STATEMENT OF CHAIRMAN JAMES LANKFORD

NOVEMBER 17, 2015

Good afternoon. I'd like to thank Chairman Perry for his willingness to hold this important joint hearing with our subcommittee. I'm hopeful that our efforts here today will shed light on how one of our top law enforcement agencies failed to protect sensitive personal information housed in internal databases.

At the outset, it is important to acknowledge the essential security role that the Secret Service fills, and its on-going dedication to our country. However, the recent history of high-profile and embarrassing scandals at the Service and the latest DHS Inspector General findings of wrong-doing cannot be swept under the rug. The IG's investigation reveals that unauthorized database searches of protected information began during a House Oversight and Government Reform hearing in March of this year. In the days that followed, many at the Secret Service continued to misuse their authority to access the sensitive employment history of Chairman Jason Chaffetz. The IG's report noted 60 instances of unauthorized access to the database by 45 Secret Service employees that violated the Privacy Act as well as internal and DHS policies.

The report also noted that 18 senior Secret Service executives failed to stop the unauthorized access or inform Director Clancy about the unauthorized accesses. In fairness, the report does reflect that one Special Agent instructed her subordinates to cease accessing the database. On its face, such wide-spread violations of our law and the public's trust are deeply disturbing. The IG did not question those involved if this was the only time they have inappropriately used the database. In the internet age, everyone is concerned about the possibility that personal information could be stolen or misused.

Our elite law enforcement agencies are not above the law and those responsible must face appropriate consequences. But to me, there is also a much bigger issue for us to examine. These days millions of Americans' personal data is stored not just on databases at the Secret Service, but across many Government agencies. A GAO report released earlier this year on the Government's Federal information security showed alarming findings. From 2009 to 2014 the number of information security incidents involving personally identifiable information reported by Federal agencies has more than doubled. GAO has stated that many agencies have largely failed to fully implement the hundreds of recommendations previously made to remedy security control vulnerabilities.

These security weaknesses continue to exist in the protection of the significant personal data of millions of Americans housed by the IRS, HHS, the VA and other agencies. Just this month, the Social Security Administration's Office of the Inspector General released a report showing that the Social Security Administration paid monetary awards to 50 employees who were previously discovered to have accessed the personal information of others without authorization. Fifty Federal employees who accessed the personal information of others, without authorization and yet incredibly in the end they were rewarded despite breaking the law. In another troublesome example, the Senate Homeland Security Committee received testimony this year that a whistleblower was retaliated against for shedding light on inadequate suicide prevention practices at a V.A. hospital.

This whistleblower learned that V.A. employees illegally and improperly accessed his private medical records after he brought to light the shameful behavior occurring at the V.A. hospital where he served. So it's not just the Secret Service that has employees who illegally accessed private information, this behavior has occurred across Government. The question is how do we fix this problem so that Americans believe that Government will protect their information and not use it to for nefarious means? I am hopeful today we can take a step forward to address this issue.

I'd like to thank Director Clancy, Inspector General Roth, and Mr. Willemssen for their testimony today. I look forward to examining these challenges with each of you.

Mr. PERRY. Chair now recognizes the Ranking Minority Member of the House Committee on Homeland Security, Subcommittee on Oversight and Management Efficiency, the gentlelady from New Jersey, Mrs. Watson Coleman, for her statement.

Mrs. WATSON COLEMAN. I want to thank you, Mr. Chairman, and Chairman Lankford, and Ranking Member Heitkamp for holding today's hearings.

Director Clancy, I want to first extend my condolences in person on the loss of your father.

Director, Inspector General Roth, and Mr. Willemssen, I thank you for your testimony. I also want to thank the men and women of the Secret Service for their diligence and hard work during the recent papal visit and the 70th anniversary of the United Nations General Assembly.

As a Member of the Committee on Homeland Security and the Committee on Oversight and Government Reform, I am well aware of the gravity of the Secret Service's mission, particularly regarding its duty to protect the President, along with foreign dignitaries, and to oversee security at major events domestically and abroad.

While I am confident that the overwhelming majority of the men and women of the Secret Service both take their jobs seriously and express the highest grade of professionalism, I am appalled by the recent reports of operational lapses and poor judgment by senior-level management.

It is obvious that there is a wide-spread lack of consistent leadership and management within Secret Service. However, this did not just begin under Director Clancy's leadership. These issues have plagued the Secret Service for a number of years.

Last year, Secretary Johnson commissioned the independent panel to evaluate the Secret Service. According to the panel's report, the Secret Service needed to undergo a cultural change, and that included having leadership that was capable of fostering greater accountability among all staff, of modernizing administrative functions including adjusting the hours special agents and uniformed division personnel must work, and improving their training.

After the panel dismantled, the inspector general continued to corroborate their findings. In 2015 alone, the inspector general has issued two memoranda regarding misconduct among senior Secret Service personnel and two Management Advisories.

The most recent Management Advisory was issued on October 21 when personnel were found sleeping on the job. The inspector general found that staffing and scheduling practices of the Secret Service contributes to officer fatigue and that this can pose immediate danger to protectees.

Instead of addressing the root of the problem of having overworked agents, the Secret Service considered the findings an isolated incident. Furthermore, the inspector general's most recent Management Advisory on improper database access of the Secret Service shows that the agency has a deeply-rooted cultural problem that is not being addressed.

The inspector general found that over 40 agents had improperly accessed the personnel records of a Member of Congress through an antiquated database.

According to the inspector general's findings, Secret Service leadership including the director and the deputy director did not recognize the severity of this situation and dismissed that data breach as a rumor.

The inspector general found that instead of dealing with this situation, the director of the Secret Service discussed the improper database access with former directors at a luncheon.

What is even far more glaring is the inspector general found that the assistant director of training, appointed by Director Clancy, to manage and direct all aspects of personnel care, development, and operational capacity training for the agencies, suggested that the information contained in this database be leaked to embarrass a Congressman.

Mr. Chairman, while this incident is reprehensible, it is not beneficial for us to be here today to speak about it in isolation. We must have a broader, productive discussion about the Secret Services' management and culture.

Finally, I know the Secret Service cannot improve without help from Congress. Therefore, I need to know too, from the director what he needs from us, to not only make the adequate changes for staffing, but also the technological advances for personal databases.

But I also need to know from the director what his plans for the agency are when he has top-level management that turns a blind eye instead of addressing issues.

With that Mr. Chairman, I yield back the balance of my time.

[The statement of Ranking Member Watson Coleman follows:]

STATEMENT OF RANKING MEMBER BONNIE WATSON COLEMAN

NOVEMBER 17, 2015

I also want to thank the men and women of the Secret Service for their diligence and hard work during the recent Papal Visit and the 70th Anniversary of the United Nations General Assembly. As a Member of the Committee on Homeland Security and the Committee on Oversight and Government Reform, I am well aware of the gravity of the Secret Service's mission, particularly regarding its duty to protect the President along with foreign dignitaries, and to oversee security at major events domestically and abroad.

While I am confident that the overwhelming majority of the men and women of the Secret Service both take their jobs seriously and express the highest grade of professionalism, I am appalled by the recent reports of operational lapses and poor judgment by senior-level management.

It is obvious that there is a wide-spread lack of consistent leadership and management within the Secret Service. However, this did not just begin under Director Clancy's leadership. These issues have plagued the Secret Service for a number of years. Last year, Secretary Johnson commissioned an independent panel to evaluate the Secret Service.

According to the Panel's report, the Secret Service needed to undergo a cultural change, and that included having leadership that was capable of fostering greater accountability among all staff, of modernizing administrative functions, including adjusting the hours Special Agents and Uniformed Division personnel must work, and improving their training.

After the panel dismantled, the inspector general continued to corroborate their findings. In 2015 alone, the inspector general has issued two memoranda regarding misconduct among senior Secret Service personnel and two management advisories.

The most recent management advisory was issued on October 21, when personnel were found sleeping on the job. The inspector general found that staffing and scheduling practices of the Secret Service contributes to officer fatigue and this could pose immediate danger to protectees. Instead of addressing the root of the problem of having overworked agents, the Secret Service considered the findings an isolated incident.

Furthermore, the inspector general's most recent management advisory on Improper Database Access at the Secret Service shows that the agency has a deeply-rooted cultural problem that is not being addressed. The inspector general found that over 40 agents improperly accessed the personnel records of a Member of Congress, through an antiquated database.

According to the inspector general's findings, Secret Service leadership including the director and the deputy director did not recognize the severity of the situation and dismissed the data breach as a rumor. The inspector general found that instead of dealing with the situation, the director of the Secret Service discussed the improper database access with former directors at a luncheon.

What is even far more glaring is the inspector general found that the assistant director of training—appointed by Director Clancy to manage and direct all aspects of personnel career development and operational capacity training for the agency-suggested that the information contained in this database be leaked to embarrass the Congressman.

Mr. Chairman, while this incident is reprehensible, it is not beneficial for us to be here today to speak about it in isolation. We must have a broader, productive discussion about the Secret Service's management and culture.

Finally, I know the Secret Service cannot improve without help from Congress. Therefore, I need to know to from the director what he needs from us to not only make the adequate changes for staffing but also the technological advancements for personnel databases, but I also need to know from the director what his plans for the agency are, when he has top-level management that turns a blind eye instead of addressing issues.

Mr. PERRY. Chair thanks the gentlelady. The Chair now recognizes the Ranking Minority Member of the Senate Committee on Homeland Security and Governmental Affair's Subcommittee on Regulatory Affairs and Federal Management, the gentlelady from North Dakota, Ms. Heitkamp for any statement she may have.

Senator HEITKAMP. Thank you Chairman Perry and Chairman Lankford. Welcome Mr. Clancy, Mr. Roth, and Mr. Willemssen. I first want to say thank you to the brave men and the brave women who serve in the Secret Service. While I understand the last few months and few years have been marked by high-profile incidents of agency misconduct, I know, I know and you know the majority of our agents work hard and put their life on the line every day to protect the White House, past Presidents, Presidential candidates, and many administration officials and foreign dignitaries.

I also know first-hand as a former leader of a law enforcement agency what the bad actions of a 2 or 3 or 4 agents can do to the morale of an entire organization. I know that, just looking at the faces behind you Mr. Clancy, I know the effect that these high-profile discussions have had.

I am here in the spirit of, let's work together to make the Secret Service what the Secret Service should be, the most trusted law enforcement agency in America. Let's restore the morale of your agents. Let's work together in a management collaboration and cooperation to change this dynamic and once again, have your agents stand tall if they tell their friends and their neighbors that they work for the Secret Service.

That is a big part of why I am here today—is to remember and remind I think everyone on this day that there are literally thousands of men and women who every day walk alongside cars, willing to sacrifice their life in protection of leaders of this country. Nothing that can be done by one person can take away the bravery of those men and women.

So clearly, we have some issues to discuss, there is no doubt about it. Clearly, you have already heard the concerns that we have here today. But my reason for being here and for being interested in this topic is really to restore the morale and restore the integrity of the Secret Service so that all the brave men and women who have done nothing wrong in the Secret Service can once again hold their heads high.

So with that, I yield back the balance of my time.

Mr. PERRY. Chair thanks the gentlelady. The Chair now recognizes the Ranking Minority Member of the House Committee on Homeland Security. The gentleman from Mississippi, Mr. Thompson for his statement.

Mr. THOMPSON. Thank you very much, Mr. Chairman. I thank the Oversight and Management Efficiency's Subcommittee and the Senate Subcommittee on Regulatory Affairs and Federal Management for holding today's hearing. I also welcome Director Clancy and Inspector General Roth and Director Willemssen today.

I join my colleagues who have already said before me, in thanking the men and women of the Secret Service for their work, during both the papal visit and the 70th anniversary of the United Nations. The dedication of the agents and officers of the Secret Service is admirable.

Unfortunately, their tireless work is time and again overshadowed by the exposure of symptomatic problems within the agency. The issues that lie within the Secret Service existed long before Director Clancy's appointment. However, as head of the agency, Congress, the public, and officers and agents he leads, hold him accountable.

Prior to Director Clancy's appointment, serious operational lapses and leadership failures led to Secretary Johnson's appointment of a independent panel to review the Secret Service. This panel, known as the Protective Mission Panel, had several glaring findings and recommendations.

One of these findings is what I have realized and articulated through many years of oversight of the Secret Service: The law enforcement agency needs to undergo a cultural change that includes leadership that is capable of fostering greater accountability.

The panel stated, "The agency is starved for leadership." Unfortunately, is still seems that as if the Secret Service has yet to be fed.

Since the Protective Mission panel completed its review, the Office of the Inspector General has led investigations into misconduct involving Secret Service supervisors on more than one occasion.

The inspector general found that in March, at least 4 supervisors turned a blind eye when 2 veteran agents, including the head of the President's protective detail, disrupted a bomb investigation by allegedly driving impaired through a barricade at the White House.

Last month, the inspector general found that at least 45 agents improperly accessed a 1980s mainframe database to retrieve information in an attempt to embarrass a Member of Congress. Of those agents who may have broken the law by improperly accessing this database, approximately 18 of them were at the GS–15 and SES levels.

The findings also concluded the director of the Secret Service, his deputy director and his chief of staff failed to take seriously that agents were discussing information about the Congressman's personnel file.

The inspector general also made the finding that the assistant director of training—the person appointed by Director Clancy to manage and direct all aspects of personnel, career development, and professionalism—suggested that the information found in the database be leaked in retaliation to Congressional oversight.

The IG's findings further illustrate that there is a lack of leadership and accountability from the top down. In this instance, very little leadership and accountability was shown. Director Clancy has indicated that the Secret Service will be expanding and undergoing a rigorous and necessary hiring phase. The new hires will be looking to their leaders for guidance.

As the Secret Service expands, it is our responsibility as Members of Congress to assist the Secret Service with adequate, necessary funding for its mission. Both the Protective Mission panel and the inspector general, have indicated that officer fatigue can place protectees at risk.

The agency also needs to have the capacity to properly vet employees before they begin work rather than continuing the practice of having uncleared personnel working in sensitive areas such as the White House.

The new recruits should represent America and have opportunities for advancement. As of right now, the Secret Service's direct diversity numbers are dismal. Furthermore, it would be hard for the law enforcement agency's commitment to equal opportunity and inclusion to be taken seriously with a class-action, racial-discrimination lawsuit still hanging over the Secret Service's head, and the Secret Service using every delay tactic it can instead of resolving the lawsuit amicably.

There must be some sweeping changes made at the Secret Service. I know the deeply-rooted problems will not cease overnight, but we must get to the source of them instead of continuously glossing over, putting on Band-Aids, and going forward with business as usual.

I look forward to working with the Secret Service to advance its mission. With that I yield back.

Mr. PERRY. Chair thanks the gentleman. The Chairman reminds other Members of the subcommittee that opening statements may be submitted for the record.

We are pleased to have a distinguished panel of witnesses before us today on this important topic. The witnesses' entire written statements will appear in the record.

The Chair will introduce all of the witnesses first and then recognize each of you for your testimony.

Mr. Joseph Clancy was appointed director of the United States Secret Service in February 2015, after serving as acting director since October 2014. Previously, Mr. Clancy served as the special agent in charge of the Presidential Protective division. Mr. Clancy began his career with the Secret Service in 1984 in the Philadelphia field office.

Welcome.

The Honorable John Roth assumed the post of inspector general for the Department of Homeland Security in March 2014. Previously, Mr. Roth served as the director of the Office of Criminal Investigations at the Food and Drug Administration and as an assistant U.S. attorney for the Eastern District of Michigan.

Welcome, Mr. Roth.

Mr. Joel Willemssen is managing director for the information technology issues at the Government Accountability Office, the GAO, where he leads the GAO's evaluations of information technology across the Federal Government.

Since joining GAO in 1979, he has led numerous reviews of information technology systems and management at a variety of Federal agencies.

Welcome, Joel.

Thank you for being here today. The Chair now recognizes Mr. Clancy for his opening statement.

STATEMENT OF JOSEPH P. CLANCY, DIRECTOR, UNITED STATES SECRET SERVICE, U.S. DEPARTMENT OF HOMELAND SECURITY

Mr. CLANCY. Good morning, Mr. Chairman, Chairman Lankford, Chairman Perry, Chairman Johnson, Ranking Member Watson Coleman, and Ranking Member Thompson, and distinguished Members of the committee.

Thank you for the opportunity to testify today. I plan to address the findings from the recent OIG report and the many improvements implemented over the past year designed to address the Protective Mission Panel findings.

I also look forward to discussing the numerous organizational changes we have made at the United States Secret Service, and would like to express my gratitude and recognize the support of Secretary Johnson and the Congress in making many of these changes possible.

I sit before you today a proud representative of the thousands of men and women who selflessly execute the mission of this agency on a daily basis. Recent accomplishments, including 4 near-simultaneous Special Security Events surrounding the papal visit and the United Nations General Assembly, as well as a number of high-profile cyber investigations serve to reinforce this feeling.

In fact, in addition to initiating protection of two Presidential candidates last week, Secret Service personnel are at this very moment deployed around the world ensuring the President's safety while in Southeast Asia in yet another example of their commitment and dedication to the mission.

Despite the Secret Service's many recent successes, I recognize that the primary reason we are here today is to address the misconduct detailed in the OIG's report. This investigation arose from allegations that the Secret Service employees inappropriately utilized an internal database to access the applicant record of an individual who is now a Member of Congress.

The misconduct outlined in the report is inexcusable and unacceptable. This conduct is not supportive of the agency's unique position of public trust. On behalf of the men and women of the Secret Service, I would like to publicly renew my apology for this breach of trust and affirm my commitment to restoring it.

The OIG reported that these employees violated existing Secret Service and DHS policies pertaining to the handling of the Privacy-Act-protected information. At the time that these violations occurred, relevant policies and procedures were in place and could be found in a number of locations, including the Secret Service Ethics Guide, the Table of Penalties, policy manuals and required on-line training courses. I was angered by the willful disregard of these policies and I am determined to ensure that all employees are held to the highest standards of professional conduct.

As I stated on prior occasions, I am committed to ensuring the accountability in this matter regardless of rank or seniority. Secretary Johnson and I stand together on this point. To date, several dozen employees have been issued disciplinary proposals relating to these events. More are on the way. The discipline is being administered in accordance with DHS and Secret Service policy, and I am confident that these actions will be fair, appropriate, and completed in a timely fashion.

A contributing factor that allowed multiple individuals to improperly access this information was the nature of the information system that housed the data. Secret Service recognized this deficiency some years ago and began a process to modernize its IT infrastructure to allow for such data to be compartmentalized and restrict the access to those with an official need to know. This process was completed this past June.

At this time, the MCI system has been officially retired. With respect to applicant records, the number of employees with access to the new system has been reduced by more than 95 percent.

Finally, much has been made of my statements and a decision of the OIG to reopen the investigation on October 5, 2015. Prior to publicly releasing the report on September 30, the OIG provided a draft copy for my review which reflected my statement that I became aware of the rumor on April 1.

As my colleagues and I reviewed the draft, I was reminded that I had, in fact, been made aware of the rumor on March 25. However, let me be clear that what I was made aware of was a rumor with no indication of employees' misconduct or employees accessing internal databases. In order to ensure the accuracy of the report and knowing the concern it would cause, I took the initiative to contact Mr. Roth prior to the report's publication to ensure the report was accurate and correct on this point.

With respect to the recommendations of the Protective Mission Panel, tremendous progress has been made in all areas. I am proud to say that we have significantly altered the way the Secret Service is structured and managed. We have also made strides in hiring new members of our workforce and expanding training opportunities for current members.

I am also realistic in knowing that many of the changes we are making will take time and that we must continue to communicate these changes to our workforce.

In the interest of time, I will point you to my written testimony submitted in advance of this hearing for a more thorough description of this process and look forward to discussing our progress on these recommendations with each of you today.

I would like to close by remembering a remarkable leader and true friend, former Assistant Director Jerry Parr. Jerry is widely known for the decisive actions he took during the March 30, 1981, assassination attempt on President Ronald Reagan. The decisions he made that day, including evacuating the President directly to the hospital, likely saved the life of the President. As I reflected on his passing, I had the opportunity to review a speech he made to a graduating special agent training class in 1994.

He stated, "An organizational culture is a product of time, successes, sufferings, failures and just plain hard work. After a hundred years or so, deep roots are developed and a corporate memory evolves. While another agency can purchase persons, equipment and technology similar to the Secret Service, it cannot buy this corporate memory. This is a priceless commodity."

As the men and women of this agency traverse these challenging times, it is important to remember that culture involves more than an agency's failures and that the successes derived from hard work and dedication will prevail as the lasting corporate memory of the Secret Service.

Thank you and I welcome any questions you may have.

[The prepared statement of Mr. Clancy follows:]

PREPARED STATEMENT OF JOSEPH P. CLANCY

NOVEMBER 17, 2015

Good afternoon, Chairman Lankford, Chairman Perry, Ranking Member Heitkamp, Ranking Member Watson Coleman, and distinguished Members of the committees. Thank you for the opportunity to testify today. I look forward to discussing the on-going challenges at the United States Secret Service ("Secret Service") including those recently outlined by the Department of Homeland Security ("DHS") Office of Inspector General ("OIG"). I am also prepared to elaborate on the organizational changes and improvements implemented over the past year to address them. I would like to express my gratitude and recognize the support of Congress in making many of these changes possible.

I proudly sit before you today representing the thousands of men and women who selflessly execute the mission of this agency on a daily basis. Over the past 150 years, the Secret Service has established itself as one of the most highly-regarded law enforcement agencies in the world. Throughout our history, we have continued to answer the call to serve our country, and through our work, have created a tradition of excellence. The cornerstone of our success is the absolute dedication to duty displayed by the men and women of this agency.

INVESTIGATION INTO THE IMPROPER ACCESS OF A SECRET SERVICE DATA SYSTEM

I would like at the outset to address the recent investigation by the DHS OIG into allegations that Secret Service employees improperly accessed and distributed information in internal databases. The investigation found that a number of employees violated existing Secret Service and DHS policies pertaining to the unauthorized access and disclosure of information protected by the Privacy Act of 1974. The behavior these employees exhibited is unacceptable. I am angered by the underlying actions reflected in the OIG's findings and am committed to ensuring that all employees are held to the highest standards of professional conduct, whether on- or off-duty. Those we protect and the public we serve expect us to live by our oaths and the values we have established as an agency, and we should demand nothing less from each other. We are better than the actions illustrated in this report and people will be held accountable for their actions. We have made necessary changes to technology in order to limit the potential for future misconduct, and are implementing enhanced training. I will continue to review policies, practices, and training to address employee misconduct and demand the highest level of integrity of all our employees.

Accountability

On behalf of the men and women of the Secret Service, I would like to publicly renew my apology for this breach of trust and confidence and state my commitment to restoring it. I have heard loud and clear the demand for accountability and need for timely, decisive discipline—and I agree. I also understand that apologies and expressions of anger are not enough. Secretary Jeh Johnson and I stand together on this point. Appropriate discipline is being administered in accordance with DHS and Secret Service policy. I am confident that the actions regarding the individuals involved will be prompt, fair, and appropriate.

Technology

On March 24, 2015, there were technological security deficiencies within the Secret Service's primary internal database that contributed to the unauthorized access of information. These internal vulnerabilities have been addressed and the potential for similar misconduct in the future mitigated. The Master Central Index ("MCI") was a mainframe application developed in 1984 that served as a central searching application and case management system. More specifically, MCI contained records from protective, investigative, and human capital divisions and served as a single access point for investigators and administrators. A significant deficiency of this arrangement was that an MCI user had access to all of the data in MCI regardless of whether it was necessary for that user's job function or not.

The Secret Service's Information Integration and Technology Transformation ("IITT") program was established in fiscal year 2010. In recognition of the limitations of MCI and other mainframe applications, the Secret Service initiated the Mainframe Application Refactoring ("MAR") project in 2011 to assess the existing 48 applications residing on the mainframe and migrate necessary capabilities and accompanying data to a non-mainframe, secure, highly-available and compartmentalized environment. DHS estimated the project would take 10 years to complete. The Secret Service accelerated the MAR project in 2013 and was able to achieve project closure on June 24, 2015. At that time, all employee mainframe access was revoked. The new systems are completely operational, and all legacy data has been migrated to new platforms where data is locked down and access to data is dependent upon job function. Protective, investigative, and human capital records reside in different systems and internal controls have now been implemented to restrict access to those systems in two ways. Now access is: (1) Limited to the respective directorates responsible for the information; and/or (2) based on the role of the system user within the organization. Shutdown of MCI began at the end of July, and it was fully powered down on August 12, 2015. Disassembly of the mainframe began in August, and it was physically removed from the data center on September 16, 2015.

Training

The OIG report also cited the need for improved and more frequent training related to unauthorized access of sensitive data. We have been working to reiterate and reinforce existing policies and training. This includes the long-standing, existing policy regarding the proper access to databases and handling of Privacy Act protected information, which is clearly stated in the Secret Service Ethics Guide, in the Table of Penalties, and within the Secret Service Manual sections related to rules of behavior with respect to the use of information technology. Employees are required to certify annually that they have reviewed these manual sections.

At the time of the conduct in question, the Secret Service was already providing a 1-hour briefing to Special Agent and Uniformed Division Training Classes that includes material on the Privacy Act. A senior Government Information Specialist from the Freedom of Information Act and Privacy Act Branch of the Office of Government and Public Affairs teaches the class and focuses, in part, on PII, with comprehensive instructional material on the subject added to the content in approximately 2012. A 1-hour in-service on-line training titled "IT Security Awareness" is required as part of the agency's adherence to the Federal Information Security Management Act ("FISMA"). The course outlines the role of Federal employees in the protection of information and in ensuring the secure operation of Federal information systems. The Privacy Act is also discussed during in-service ethics classes administered to the field by Secret Service Office of Chief Counsel instructors. Further, DHS requires Secret Service employees to complete annual in-service on-line training titled, "Privacy at DHS: Protecting Personal Information." This training was incorporated into the required curriculum in 2012 and covers proper handling of PII. While the class is annually required, due to the gravity of the findings in the OIG report, I instructed the workforce in an official message on October 16 to retake the class by November 30.

Additionally, at my direction enhanced briefings regarding the Privacy Act are now being provided to Special Agent and Uniformed Division Training Classes by Office of Chief Counsel instructors. A permanent curriculum is being developed and a formal class for candidate and in-service employee training is anticipated in the near future.

Finally, I would like to address my statements and the decision of the OIG to reopen the investigation on October 5, 2015. Prior to the public release of the report on September 30, 2015, the OIG provided me a draft electronic copy of the report for review. I received this draft report from the OIG during the National Special Security Events ("NSSEs") in New York City associated with the Pope's visit and the UN General Assembly. During the process of reviewing the draft, I was reminded by a colleague that I had been informed of a rumor regarding the individual's application history on March 25. While I myself do not recall hearing of this rumor, several others have confirmed that I did, and that it was a general rumor about the individual's past application; it did not relate to USSS employees improperly accessing databases or sharing protected information. In order to ensure accuracy within the report, on my own initiative I contacted the OIG to correct the record. I did not make the decision to contact the OIG blindly and was fully aware that additional scrutiny would result from my doing so. I made this decision because I feel that it is important to be as forthcoming, accurate, and complete as possible. I expect this from my employees and expect nothing less from myself.

The OIG published an addendum in October reporting its assessment of the updated information pertaining to when I was made aware of this rumor. Interviews with former directors, my deputy director, and my former chief of staff only serve to corroborate that the information available to me at the time was nothing more than a rumor. The information was not attributed to a Secret Service data system or indicative of any action—inappropriate or otherwise—by any Secret Service employee. Nothing in the addendum contradicts what I have maintained from the beginning—that at no time prior to April 2, was I aware that potential misconduct could be the source of this rumor. When I did learn of it, I began taking immediate action, contacting the OIG and sending an official message to the workforce on the handling of sensitive information.

FULFILLING THE INDEPENDENT PROTECTIVE MISSION PANEL'S RECOMMENDATIONS

I would now like to turn to the actions we have taken to implement the recommendations of the independent Protective Mission Panel (the "Panel"), which was established by Secretary Jeh Johnson following the events of September 19, 2014 to undertake a broad review of the Secret Service's protection of the White House complex. The Panel's work, aided by full cooperation of the Secret Service and DHS, concluded with the publication of the *Report from the United States Secret Service Protective Mission Panel to the Secretary of Homeland Security* (the "Report"), issued on December 15, 2014.

The Report memorialized the findings and recommendations of the Panel in three general areas: Training and Personnel; Technology, Perimeter Security, and Operations; and Leadership. Upon receipt of the Report, the Secret Service acknowledged and accepted the Panel's findings and recommendations. A number of the issues found in the review were recognized independently prior to the issuance of the Report and were being addressed, while those that remained were prioritized and incorporated into a strategic action plan designed to fully implement the Panel's findings as time and resources permitted.

I am proud to say that we have significantly altered the way the Secret Service is structured and managed since my return to the agency. We have also made strides in hiring new members of our workforce, and in expanding training opportunities for current members. I am also realistic in knowing that the changes we are making will take time to realize their full impact, particularly as they relate to staffing levels, and that we must continue to communicate these changes to our workforce. Some of the PMP recommendations will never be closed, as they require a commitment to on-going evaluation, innovation, and continuous improvement. I am hopeful that the structural changes we have made to the Secret Service will foster an environment where this perspective is not only valued, but also encouraged. I am committed to this process and am certain that the Secret Service will emerge a stronger agency with the continued support of the Department, the administration, and the Congress.

Training and Personnel

I recognized early on in my tenure that many of the most serious problems facing the Secret Service can be traced back to inadequate staffing levels. Achieving appropriate staffing levels will allow the workforce to undertake a level of training commensurate with the mission and help to address the resultant effect on morale. Once underway, the process is, to some extent, self-repairing in that as morale improves, attrition rates will fall and staffing levels will continue to increase toward desired levels.

In May 2015, to address staffing issues and following a wider professionalization initiative in which I placed civilian specialists in executive-level leadership positions, I implemented a reorganization effort aimed at more efficiently recruiting and hiring special agents, Uniformed Division ("UD") officers, and administrative, professional, and technical ("APT") personnel. Both the Human Capital and Recruitment Divisions were closed and their collective responsibilities were redistributed to a number of new divisions. The Talent and Employee Acquisition Management Division ("TAD") is one such division, and this reorganization has allowed its managers to focus exclusively on recruiting and hiring diverse applicants to fill special agent, UD, and APT positions. In the ensuing months, TAD has implemented a modern recruitment strategy, including embracing social media as a recruiting tool and budgeting fiscal year ("FY") 2016 dollars towards an aggressive advertising campaign aimed at attracting qualified applicants to the agency. Further, in order to avoid bottlenecks and streamline the process of on-boarding qualified applicants, the Secret Service is hiring contractors to serve as a stop-gap solution for reviewing hiring qualifications through TAD and monitoring background investigations through the Security Clearance Division ("SCD") until an adequate number of APTs can be hired and trained to perform these functions.

Identifying our needs is a key element of supporting appropriate staffing levels because it drives our budget requests and justifications. In July, we completed the U.S. Secret Service Human Capital Plan for fiscal year 2015 through 2019. This foundational document identifies our strategy for increasing staffing levels, by accounting for mission, training, and work/life balance requirements. Consistent with the results of the PMP, our analysis suggests that staffing levels must significantly increase over the next 5 years to support not only our mission requirements but also our employee training and work/life balance needs. We look forward to continuing our work with the Department and Congress to secure the financial resources necessary to support these enhanced staffing levels.

In response to the PMP recommendation that the Secret Service increase the number of personnel assigned to UD and the Presidential Protective Division ("PPD"), we worked closely with the Federal Law Enforcement Training Center ("FLETC") to schedule 10 special agent classes with 195 agents and 8 UD classes with 151 officers in fiscal year 2015, a significant increase from years immediately preceding. Additionally, in fiscal year 2016, we have again asked FLETC for increased numbers of trainee classes and hope to bring 12 special agent and 12 UD classes on board this year. Today, the recommended personnel increase to PPD is substantially complete, while efforts to reach net gains that approach recommended levels in UD continue in the face of greater challenges with respect to attrition and retention. Given this challenge, the Secret Service recently introduced a UD retention bonus and is engaged with the Department to develop additional programs designed to incentivize members of our talented workforce to refrain from separating prematurely from the agency.

A number of the Panel's recommendations were directed to training, including conducting integrated training in realistic conditions, and an increase in the overall amount of training received by agents and officers assigned to protective functions. The Secret Service has worked diligently to implement integrated training between the various units assigned to the White House complex. Currently, 99% of UD officers and technicians have completed specially created "Emergency Action/Building Defense" training. Training for agents assigned to permanent protective details has also increased with special agents on the Presidential Protective Division receiving approximately 25% more training in fiscal year 2015 than in fiscal year 2014. In order to more realistically simulate the conditions in which our agents, officers, and technicians operate, our fiscal year 2016 budget request includes funds directed to the design and construction of a more permanent White House training facility. Additionally, as staffing levels increase, the number of training hours that personnel assigned to UD and protective details receive will continue to increase accordingly. I firmly believe that, given the nature of the Secret Service's integrated mission, the importance of the amount and quality of training provided to our workforce cannot be overstated.

Technology, Perimeter Security, and Operations

For the purposes of today's hearing, I will speak generally to the Panel's recommendations on technology and perimeter security. The Panel believed strongly, as do I, that operational issues related to the protection of the White House should not be the subject of a detailed public debate in their report or any other fora. I pledge to continue to provide you and your staffs with relevant information in the proper setting, at your request, as we move forward implementing these recommendations. My No. 1 priority has been, and is, the protection of the President, Vice President, and their families.

To address longer-range future technology needs, the Secret Service will continue to partner with the Department's Science and Technology Directorate, the Department of Defense, and our partners in the intelligence community to ensure we are researching, developing, and deploying cutting-edge technology.

The Secret Service has recognized the need for protective enhancements to the White House complex fence and is currently working with stakeholders to create a viable, long-term solution. This multi-phase project began with the formation of requirements that are guiding a formal study aimed at identifying various fence options. These requirements encompassed security concerns identified by the Secret Service, including efforts to delay intruders, as well as aesthetic and historic concerns put forward by the National Park Service ("NPS").

Working at a highly accelerated pace with the National Capital Planning Commission ("NCPC"), the U.S. Commission of Fine Arts, and the NPS, the Secret Service was able to not only secure approval for, but also complete the installation of an interim improvement to the fence that inhibits the ability of individuals to climb it. We also worked with NPS to complete a study to identify the options for permanent enhancements to perimeter security earlier this year. We are moving forward with the design phase of this project, and look forward to working with the NCPC to secure its approval in early 2016.

Leadership

The majority of the recommendations contained in the Report fell under the category of "Leadership." Dynamic leadership that encourages open communication, rewards innovation, values flexibility, rejects insularity, and embraces personal accountability is vital to the agency's long-term success. Based upon the Panel's review, and my own assessments, I implemented several leadership changes in the Secret Service executive management team earlier this year. These changes were necessary to gain a fresh perspective on how we conduct business. The Panel's recommendations on leadership have been incorporated into the strategic action plan referenced above.

The Panel recommended that the agency should promote specialized expertise in its budget, workforce, and technology functions. This assessment has been embraced, and, through a professionalization initiative, many executive positions formerly held by career law enforcement agents are now held by civilians with the training and experience necessary to effectively guide an organization of this size. First and foremost, we established a new chief operating officer (COO) position, a non-law enforcement Senior Executive Service (SES)-level position that is equivalent to the deputy director. Along with the creation of this position, we elevated the Office of the Chief Financial Officer (CFO) to a directorate-level entity, created the Office of Strategic Planning and Policy (OSP), and split the Office of Human Resources and Training (HRT) into two directorate-level offices—the Office of Human Resources (HUM) and the Office of Training (TNG). By splitting HRT into two directorates, we are expecting to achieve greater focus on two key areas of concern for the PMP—staffing and training. In the revised organizational structure, the CFO, HUM, OSP, and the chief information officer (CIO) are now aligned under the COO. We will continue to evaluate our organizational structure and make changes where it is necessary.

In addition to the structural changes, we used this opportunity to evaluate the skills required for directorate-level leadership positions to examine which would be best filled by non-law enforcement professionals. As a result of this examination, three of our ten directorates are led by non-law enforcement professionals, including the CFO, OSP, and our Office of Technical Development and Mission Support (TEC). Further, we have enhanced our executive-level perspective by appointing non-law enforcement professionals to the SES-level roles of CIO, deputy CIO, and component acquisition executive (CAE), and are in the process of hiring for a newly-created SES-level director of communications position.

One of the principal responsibilities of the CFO has been to start the process for developing a zero-based budget as recommended by the panel. This enormous undertaking is underway, and it is my hope that a mission-based budget will begin to be implemented in the fiscal year 2018 budget cycle. Important steps have been taken in furtherance of this goal, including the development of the previously mentioned Human Capital Plan, and benchmarking Secret Service analytical capabilities, staff resources, and planning activities with comparable organizations.

A common theme within the panel's recommendations on leadership was the need for improved internal and external communication. I wholly adopt this view and firmly believe that improved communication is directly related to increased effectiveness and morale. I have affirmed this priority to the executive management team, and my expectation and message to them is that they do the same within their directorates. The agency's priorities have been communicated externally through active engagement with the Department, the administration, and Congress. This outreach will continue, and future operational and managerial decisions will be guided by these priorities.

Internally, I have personally visited many of our field offices, all former Presidential protective details, and conducted video-conferenced town hall meetings with the agency's workforce. I have joined officers and agents at the White House complex and the Vice-President's residence during their daily roll call. Earlier this year, I met with field supervisors for an Investigative Issues Focus Group to obtain a better understanding of the issues and concerns of the agents in the field. I plan to continue to have an open and honest conversation with members of our workforce about their concerns and discuss what I can do to address them.

As part of our outreach to employees, we conducted a Work/Life Assessment through a third-party contractor. The results of the 47 focus groups conducted under this effort provided us with a roadmap that allowed us to identify and begin to act upon the concerns of our workforce. In terms of delivering information, we have started sending important email messages to affected employees' individual inboxes, which allows them much easier access to information than was previously available only via official messages accessible exclusively through a networked connection to the Secret Service email server. Additionally, we have started to leverage multimedia in our approach, including creating videos to communicate major policy changes and initiatives. Finally, just weeks ago, we launched a new web-based platform, Spark!, which we expect will enhance two-way communication between the workforce and leadership by providing a forum to raise ideas, suggestions, and concerns. Employees should have every assurance that I will continue to work to share information and feel it is my responsibility to find solutions to the issues or concerns they voice.

Accountability is another issue that I believe the Panel was rightly focused on due to its effects on workforce morale and operational readiness. Even before the Panel issued its recommendations, as a result of a number of incidents involving personal conduct, my predecessors had already taken important steps to address these issues. These steps were intended to increase transparency, consistency, and fairness in disciplinary actions and included the following:

- A Professionalism Reinforcement Working Group ("PRWG") was initiated to conduct an objective and comprehensive review of the agency's values and professional standards of conduct;
- As a result of the PRWG, we created and published a comprehensive ethics guide, initiated an active schedule of ethics training, conducted integrity training, and implemented a new centralized disciplinary policy including a Table of Penalties (issued on 11/15/2013);
- An "Inspection Hotline" was created and prominently displayed on the Secret Service's Intranet Home page for employees to report misconduct to the Secret Service Office of Professional Responsibility or the DHS OIG and allow the

agency or the Department to initiate swift investigative or administrative action;

- Extensive training requirements for new supervisors were created. Training includes mandatory completion of the DHS leadership development program and the agency's 40-hour, classroom-based Management and Emerging Leaders seminars. The requirements also include the assignment of a senior-level mentor to guide supervisors in the first year of their assignment;
- The chief integrity officer position was established, and we reinforced the importance of leadership and accountability with supervisors and provided developmental training to over 5,000 employees; and
- The ITG created a Discipline Analysis Report for Calendar Year 2014, which we posted for all employees to view on our intranet site. The posting of this report was the first time the Secret Service made this type of data available for review by the workforce and underscores our commitment to support a culture of transparency within our workforce. We made this decision in response to the concerns raised by the workforce regarding the consistency and fairness of our discipline process.

As recommended by the Panel, we firmly believe that we can further enhance and improve our performance by partnering with other organizations to collect their best practices and leverage their knowledge. We have greatly expanded our outreach efforts to learn from the Department of Defense and intelligence community, particularly in the areas of training and technology.

In the area of training, the Secret Service completed a number of joint training exercises with entities that included representatives from the military, Federal, State, and local law enforcement and other protective agencies. Our employees benefited from the perspective of the Department of Defense community during training opportunities at their facilities. In other cases, like the security planning and preparation preceding the Papal visit last month, our employees had a chance to examine protective methodologies while observing security officials from the Vatican. These efforts were in addition to the opportunity to work with the security personnel who traveled with the world leaders that attended the 70th United Nations General Assembly.

The Secret Service also has benefited from both existing and newly-established relationships within the interagency and intelligence communities and with the Department of Defense related to technology. A few examples where we are currently leveraging these relationships include the challenges with unmanned aerial vehicles ("UAV") and gunshot detection.

While the above summarizes our activities in a number of areas, the totality of the actions we have taken since receiving the recommendations of the PMP is substantial. Secret Service employees at every level have been working hard not only to support our mission requirements, but also to establish the foundation for significant changes that will positively impact the Secret Service over the long-term.

MISSION EXCELLENCE

In addition to working on the implementation of the Panel's recommendations, one of my biggest priorities over the past year has been to restore the Secret Service's reputation of mission excellence. Thousands of special agents, uniformed officers, and civilian staff successfully fulfill the integrated mission of this agency every day throughout the world.

It is important to remember that protection is only a portion of the integrated mission of the Secret Service. The expertise, maturity, and judgment special agents develop as criminal investigators conducting counterfeit currency, financial, or cyber crime investigations are essential to the extremely critical and demanding work of protecting our Nation's highest elected leaders, as well as those world leaders who travel to our country.

Just 2 months ago, members of the Secret Service came together from field offices across the country and throughout the world to successfully execute security plans at 4, near-simultaneous NSSEs while also protecting President Xi Jingping of China during his first state visit to the United States. The planning for the 4 NSSEs spanned over 8 months. This is the first time in the history of the agency—or this country—that such a feat has been accomplished.

The 4 NSSEs involved a monumental three city tour of Pope Francis to Washington, DC, Philadelphia, PA, and New York, NY, as well as the 70th United Nations General Assembly. Agency personnel coordinated security plans for the President, Vice-President, Pope, and approximately 160 heads of state and over 80 spouses.

In addition to honing personnel who are able to serve as specialists in the planning and staffing of protective operations, the integrated mission serves another purpose. Agents in the field also forge strong relationships with local law enforcement partners in investigations that pay dividends when we need their assistance during a protective visit. The Secret Service has long recognized that partnerships and cooperation act as force multipliers in both our protective and investigative missions. In this instance, with the need for critical support from State and local partners, these relationships proved to be invaluable.

Plans for the NSSEs in September involved bringing together 2,500 additional Federal law enforcement officers from other Federal agencies, the support of dozens of State and local law enforcement organizations, screening over 1 million people, and securing over 25 individual sites including the United States Capitol, Central Park and Madison Square Garden in New York, and the Benjamin Franklin Parkway in Philadelphia. At the same time, preparations were underway and continue to be developed for upcoming Presidential trips with multiple stops in Asia, Presidential and Vice-Presidential candidate protection, the two National political conventions, and Presidential and Vice-Presidential debate sites.

In addition to the 4 NSSEs, the Secret Service in fiscal year 2015 conducted over 6,245 protective visits. Protective details and field agents ensured protection for over 5,981 domestic stops and approximately 264 international stops. The Secret Service Uniformed Division completed more than 677 magnetometer/X-ray operations assignments, and screened more than 2,742,620 members of the public. The Secret Service stopped approximately 2,847 weapons at magnetometer checkpoints from entering secure venues. The protective mission was also supported by over 6,617 protective surveys and approximately 136 protective intelligence arrests.

Additionally, Secret Service investigations continue to produce Nationally and internationally significant results, much of them in strong coordination with the Department of Justice, other law enforcement agencies, and our public- and private-sector partners. Two recent cases exemplify the work our agents do daily, in order to protect our Nation's financial infrastructure.

In October, the Secret Service worked to apprehend and extradite yet another alleged cyber criminal—Sergey Vovnenko. Vovnenko is charged with conspiring to hack into the computer networks of individual users and corporations to steal login credentials and payment card data. According to the indictment, for almost 2 years, Vovnenko and his conspirators operated an international criminal organization that stole data, including user names and passwords for bank accounts and other online services, as well as debit and credit card numbers and personally identifiable information. To carry out this crime, Vovnenko allegedly operated a "botnet" of more than 13,000 computers infected with malicious computer software programmed to gain unauthorized access to other computers and to identify, store, and export information from hacked computers.

In the same week that Vovnenko appeared in Federal court in Newark, the Secret Service, in coordination with its partners in the Peruvian National Police, arrested 4 suspects with ties to the production and transportation of counterfeit U.S. currency. At the time of the arrests, the suspects were traveling to the airport en route the United States and allegedly possessed close to $850,000 of counterfeit U.S. currency skillfully secreted in suitcase liners. According to Secret Service records, one of the particular types of counterfeit notes seized in this case has a passing history exceeding $34 million dating back to 2009. These are just two examples of the agency's highly successful investigative work for which hard-working personnel should be commended.

CONCLUSION

As I look back over the past year, I see an agency in the midst of reform. I wish that people could walk in my shoes for a day and see what I see—a workforce with an uncompromising sense of duty and commitment to its integrated mission.

Recently, the Secret Service lost a remarkable leader and true friend in former Assistant Director Jerry Parr. Jerry is widely known for the decisive actions taken during the March 30, 1981 assassination attempt on President Ronald Reagan. The decisions he made that day, including evacuating the President directly to the hospital, likely saved the life of the President. As I reflected on his passing, I had the opportunity to review a speech he made to a graduating special agent training class in 1994. In that speech he spoke of culture. He said:

"An organizational culture is a product of time, successes, sufferings, failures, and just plain hard work. After a hundred years or so, deep roots are developed, and a corporate memory evolves. While another agency can purchase persons, equipment, and technology similar to the Secret Service, it cannot buy this corporate memory. This is a priceless commodity."

As the men and women of this agency traverse these challenging times, I am heartened by the corporate memory of this great organization. I am confident that through unparalleled dedication of our personnel, and the actions we are taking to reform and improve, the Secret Service will meet the standard of excellence that we have established over our history and which our Nation's leaders and the American people rightly expect of us.

Chairman Lankford, Chairman Perry, Ranking Member Heitkamp, and Ranking Member Watson Coleman, this concludes my written testimony. I welcome any questions you have at this time.

Mr. PERRY. Thank you, Mr. Clancy.

The Chair now recognizes Mr. Roth for an opening statement.

STATEMENT OF JOHN ROTH, INSPECTOR GENERAL, OFFICE OF INSPECTOR GENERAL, U.S. DEPARTMENT OF HOMELAND SECURITY

Mr. ROTH. Chairmen Lankford, Perry, and Johnson, Ranking Members Heitkamp, Watson Coleman, and Thompson and Members of the subcommittee, thank you for inviting me here today to testify.

We have conducted a number of investigations, audits, inspections of Secret Service programs and operations, and we have a number of on-going projects. My written testimony describes some of that work and discusses its implications.

For my oral remarks, I will discuss our investigation into the allegations that the Secret Service agents improperly accessed a restricted database to discover details about Chairman Jason Chaffetz' application to the Secret Service, as well as some other on-going work.

We found that the Chaffetz application entry contained within a Secret Service database called the Master Central Index was accessed by Secret Service employees on approximately 60 occasions between March 25 and April 2 of this year. We concluded that the vast majority of those who accessed the information did so in violation of the Privacy Act of 1974, as well as Secret Service and DHS policy.

We identified one individual who acknowledged disclosing information protected by the Privacy Act to an outside source. However, because the number of individuals with access to this information was so great, we were unable to identify others who may have disclosed protected information to third parties.

We found that the access began minutes after Director Clancy began testifying before the Committee on Oversight and Government Reform on March 24, and continued in the days following. Knowledge of Chairman Chaffetz' application was wide-spread and fueled and confirmed by improper access to the Secret Service database at issue.

We found that a number of senior managers knew agents were accessing the MCI improperly and some of them accessed it themselves. Other senior managers were aware that Chairman Chaffetz once had applied at the Secret Service but they apparently did not comprehend the seriousness of what was developing. As a result, no one acted until it was too late to stop this unauthorized and unlawful activity.

Our investigation also revealed that the MCI, a case management tool implemented in 1984, did not have the audit and access controls of a modern IT system or appropriately segregate information. Such controls and segregation may have prevented or at least minimized the behavior we discovered.

This also appears to run counter to the Privacy Act which requires agencies to establish appropriate administrative, technical, and physical safeguards to ensure the safety and—I am sorry, the security and confidentiality of the records.

Additionally, the Secret Service must ensure that only relevant records are maintained in these types of databases. The Privacy Act requires that the agency maintain its records only such information about an individual as is relevant and necessary to accomplish a purpose of the agency.

The fact that the MCI had records of an unsuccessful application from 12 years earlier which contained sensitive information, the disclosure of which could lead to identity theft, may violate this provision of the Privacy Act.

Finally, although all agents were trained in the use of the system and received yearly refresher training, it was apparent that many of the agents disregarded that training.

The Secret Service recently reported that it retired the MCI and migrated all data to about 5 other Secret Service information systems in September 2015. Our Office of Information Technology Audits is currently conducting a technical security assessment of the information systems that the Secret Service now uses to store and retrieve this information. We expect to complete that assessment and issue a final report in February 2016.

Over the past year-and-a-half as part of our independent oversight effort, we have investigated various incidents involving allegations of misconduct by Secret Service employees and other issues related to the Secret Service's organization and mission. The results of our investigation and reviews point to on-going organizational and management challenges. The Secret Service has certainly taken steps to address these challenges but not always successfully.

Additionally, we are reviewing 3 incidents involving potential security lapses. For each incidence—incident—shots being fired at the White House from Constitution Avenue, an intruder jumping over the fence and entering the White House, an armed guard coming in close proximity to the President—we are determining whether the Secret Service followed its own protective policies, what actions were taken to correct, identify deficiencies and whether these corrections were adequate.

The ultimate aim of our review is to determine and understand the root causes of these lapses. This fiscal year we plan to issue 3 reports on these incidents, as well as a capping report that identifies the root causes and includes any other necessary overarching recommendations.

Mr. Chairman, this concludes my prepared statement. I welcome any questions you or any other Members of the subcommittees may have.

[The prepared statement of Mr. Roth follows:]

PREPARED STATEMENT OF JOHN ROTH

NOVEMBER 17, 2015

Chairmen Lankford and Perry, Ranking Members Heitkamp and Watson Coleman, and Members of the subcommittees: Thank you for inviting me here today to discuss our on-going work involving the United States Secret Service (Secret Service) and its Government-wide implications. We have conducted a number of investigations, audits, and inspections of Secret Service programs and operations, and we have a number of on-going projects. My testimony today will describe some of that work and discuss its implications.

ALLEGATIONS CONCERNING ACCESS TO CHAIRMAN CHAFFETZ' APPLICATION FILE

As a result of our investigation, we determined that a Secret Service database containing sensitive personally identifiable information pertaining to Congressman Jason Chaffetz, Chairman of the House Committee on Oversight and Government Reform, was accessed by Secret Service employees on approximately 60 occasions between March 25 and April 2 of this year.[1] We concluded that a vast majority of those who accessed the information did so in violation of the *Privacy Act of 1974* (Privacy Act), as well as Secret Service and Department of Homeland Security (DHS) policy. We also identified one individual who acknowledged disclosing information protected by the Privacy Act to an outside source. However, because the number of individuals with access to this information was so great, we were unable to identify others who may have disclosed protected information to third parties.

We found that the access began minutes after Director Clancy began testifying before the Committee on Oversight and Government Reform on March 24 and continued in the days following. Knowledge of Chairman Chaffetz' application was widespread and was fueled and confirmed by improper access to the Secret Service database at issue, the Master Central Index (MCI).

We found that a number of senior managers knew agents were accessing the MCI improperly. For example, the special agent in charge of the Washington Field Office (WFO) became aware on or about March 25 that several of her mid-level WFO supervisors had accessed or were aware of the Chaffetz record, and she directed her subordinates to cease any further access of the MCI record. No other Secret Service personnel at WFO accessed the Chaffetz record after that date, but 25 others around the country did. Likewise, Deputy Assistant Director Cynthia Wofford of the Office of Strategic Intelligence and Information recalled hearing rumors of the Chaffetz application during the director's March 24 testimony. After unsuccessfully searching the internet for confirmation of the rumor, Wofford accessed the MCI on the morning of March 25 and found the Chaffetz record. She attempted to bring this to the attention of Deputy Director Magaw, but he told her that he already knew about it.

However, other senior managers were aware that Chairman Chaffetz had once applied to the Secret Service, but they apparently did not comprehend the seriousness of what was developing. None of the senior managers apparently understood that the rumors were being fueled and confirmed by numerous agents who improperly accessed the protected MCI record of the Chaffetz application. As a result, no one acted, until it was too late, to stop this unauthorized and unlawful activity.

Our investigation also revealed that the MCI, a case management tool implemented in 1984 to facilitate the Secret Service's investigative process, did not have the audit and access controls of a modern information technology (IT) system or appropriately segregate the information. Such controls and segregation may have prevented or minimized the behavior we discovered. This also appears to run counter to the Privacy Act, which requires agencies to "establish appropriate administrative, technical, and physical safeguards to insure the security and confidentiality of records."

Additionally, the Secret Service must ensure that only relevant records are maintained in these types of databases. The Privacy Act requires that an agency "maintain in its records only such information about an individual as is relevant and necessary to accomplish a purpose of the agency required to be accomplished." The fact that the MCI had records of an unsuccessful application from 12 years earlier, which contained sensitive information the disclosure of which could lead to identity theft, may violate this provision of the Privacy Act. Finally, although all agents were trained on use of the system and received yearly refresher training, it was apparent that many of the agents disregarded that training.

---

[1] Memorandum, "Investigation into the Improper Access and Distribution of Information Contained Within a Secret Service Data System" (September 25, 2015).

Our Office of Information Technology Audits is currently conducting a technical security assessment of the information systems the Secret Service now uses to store and retrieve investigative and criminal history information. The Secret Service recently reported that it retired the MCI and migrated all data to about 5 other Secret Service information systems in September 2015. The objectives of our technical assessment are to verify that the MCI is no longer in use, identify which systems currently house MCI data, determine the level of physical and system controls implemented to secure the data from further instances of unauthorized access, and identify gaps in the security posture. We also intend, to the extent possible, to understand the security weaknesses in the MCI when it was operational. We expect to complete our assessment and issue a final report in February 2016.

PREVIOUS ALLEGATIONS OF EMPLOYEE MISCONDUCT

Over the past several years, as part of our independent oversight effort, we have investigated various incidents involving allegations of misconduct by Secret Service employees. We have also reviewed other issues related to the Secret Service's organization and mission that raised the concern of Congress and the public. In sum, the results of our investigations and reviews, as well as other incidents we were made aware of, point to some on-going organizational and management challenges. The Secret Service has certainly taken steps to address these challenges, but not always successfully. These persistent challenges may not be easy to resolve through expeditious action, such as suspending employees and issuing new guidance. They may require more fundamental change that addresses the root cause of the misconduct.

Allegation Into Agent Misconduct at the White House Complex on March 4, 2015

We reviewed the actions of two Secret Service agents who on the evening of March 4 had entered an area that had been secured as a result of a suspicious package.[2] We concluded that it was more likely than not that both agents' judgment was impaired by alcohol. We found that, notwithstanding their denials, both agents were observed by uniformed officers as "not right," and "not making sense," had just spent the previous 5 hours in a restaurant/bar in which one ran up a significant bar tab, and that they drove into a crime scene inches from what the rest of the Secret Service was treating as a potential explosive device and which, under different circumstances, could have endangered their own lives and those of the Uniformed Division (UD) officers responding.

While each agent had a duty to report the incident to his superior, neither did do so. We found that their failure to do so reflected either poor judgment or an affirmative desire to hide their activities.

Allegation Into Misuse of Government Resources to Conduct Employee Protection Operations

We also investigated an allegation that under an operation called "Operation Moonlight" Secret Service personnel and resources were directed to conduct surveillance and records checks unrelated to the Secret Service's mission.[3] The complaint alleged that Secret Service agents were instructed to use law enforcement databases and conduct rotating surveillance shifts on a neighbor of the then-Executive Staff Assistant to the former Secret Service Director. We did not find any instances in which Secret Service agents approached the neighbor, nor could we conclude that the neighbor's house was ever under direct surveillance.

Our ensuing investigation, however, revealed that personnel and database resources were misused when Washington Field Office "Prowler" teams periodically checked on the executive staff assistant at her residence for about 1 week in early July 2011. Our investigation also showed these checks were initiated in response to a private dispute and did not occur in the course of official duties or as a result of the executive staff assistant's position. In addition, we determined that the Prowler team agents were not investigating a potential assault on the executive staff assistant; the agents commonly described undertaking the checks because of an issue she was having with her neighbor.

Secret Service personnel told us that the Prowler team checks did not divert resources from essential functions and responsibilities or negatively impact the Secret Service's mission. However, the checks on the executive staff assistant in La Plata, Maryland—a 45-minute drive from the White House—diverted Prowler personnel

---

[2] Memorandum, "Investigation Into the Incident at the White House Complex on March 4, 2015" (May 6, 2015).

[3] Memorandum, "Allegations of Misuse of United States Secret Service Resources" (October 17, 2014).

from the White House area and its surroundings when, on 4 of 5 identified days, the President was departing, arriving, or at the White House.

Allegations of Secret Service Misconduct in Cartagena, Colombia

We also investigated allegations that, in April 2012, during preparations for President Obama's visit to Cartagena, Colombia, Secret Service agents solicited prostitutes and engaged in other misconduct.

During our investigation, we independently identified Secret Service personnel who directly supported the Cartagena visit and other potential witnesses who may have had information about the Cartagena trip. We identified the personnel directly involved in the incident, as well as the potential witnesses, through documentary sources, including official travel records, hotel registries, country clearance cables, personnel assignments, and Secret Service and U.S. Embassy records.

As part of our investigation, we conducted 283 interviews of 251 Secret Service personnel. Based on our interviews and review of records, we identified 13 Secret Service employees who had personal encounters with female Colombian nationals consistent with the misconduct reported. We determined that one of the female Colombian nationals involved in the incident was known to the intelligence community. However, we found no evidence that the actions of Secret Service personnel had compromised any sensitive information.

Our investigation determined that 12 Secret Service employees met 13 female Colombian nationals at bars or clubs and returned with them to their rooms at the Hotel Caribe or the Hilton Cartagena Hotel. In addition, one Secret Service employee met a female Colombian national at the apartment of a Drug Enforcement Administration special agent. We interviewed the remaining 12 Secret Service employees who had personal encounters with the 13 female Colombian nationals. Through our interviews, we learned that following their encounters, 3 females left the rooms without asking for money, 5 females asked for money and were paid, and 4 females asked for money but were not paid. In addition, 1 female, who asked to be paid but was not, brought a Colombian police officer to the door of the Secret Service employee's room; the employee did not answer the door. As a result, she was paid by another Secret Service employee and left. A fourteenth Secret Service employee, who the Secret Service initially identified as involved in the misconduct, was subsequently determined to have been misidentified.

Of the 13 employees accused of soliciting prostitutes in Cartagena, 3 were returned to duty with memoranda of counseling, after being cleared of serious misconduct. Five employees had their security clearance revoked because they either knowingly solicited prostitutes, demonstrated lack of candor during the investigation, or both. Five employees resigned or retired prior to the adjudication of their security clearance. Several of these last 5 employees appealed their adverse personnel actions to the United States Merit Systems Protection Board.

After the incident, the Secret Service issued new guidance regarding personal behavior, including a directive amending standards of conduct with additional policies about off-duty conduct, briefings, and supervision on foreign trips.

Other Misconduct by Secret Service Employees

Although we did not investigate them, 6 incidents that occurred between June 2013 and June 2014 highlighted questionable conduct by Secret Service employees that affected the Secret Service's protective function. These incidents took place after the Secret Service instituted new policies (in April 2012) on alcohol use, including prohibiting use within 10 hours of reporting for duty and prohibiting drinking at the protectee's hotel once a protective visit has begun (but permitting drinking "in moderate amounts" while off-duty during a protective mission).

- In June 2013, 2 UD officers were found to have consumed alcohol during an overseas mission, in violation of the 10-hour rule regarding alcohol consumption. One of the officers, a second-time offender, handled his rifle while under the influence of alcohol. He received a 28-day suspension; the other officer received a 7-day suspension.
- In November 2013, a supervisory agent was involved in an incident at the Hay Adams hotel in Washington, DC. The supervisor began conversing with a woman at the hotel bar and later accompanied the woman to her room. The woman solicited the help of hotel security when she wanted the agent to leave her room, reporting that he had a gun and she was frightened. The agent left the room without incident. The Secret Service conducted an inquiry and issued a letter of reprimand to the agent.
- In December 2013, 4 UD officers were found to have consumed alcohol during a layover on an overseas mission, in violation of the 10-hour rule regarding alco-

hol consumption. Four of these officers were issued letters of reprimand; the fifth, a second-time offender, was issued a 14-day suspension.

- In March 2014, a UD officer was involved in a car accident while driving a Government-rented vehicle during official travel supporting a Presidential visit. The officer was found to have consumed alcohol in the hours preceding the accident, in violation of the 10-hour rule regarding alcohol consumption. The officer was ultimately served with a 7-day suspension. This officer was one of 10 others who were out together the evening before the accident. Three of the other officers violated the 10-hour rule and a fourth misused a Government-rented vehicle. These officers were issued suspensions ranging from 14 days to 35 days. One of the officers resigned.
- In March 2014, an agent was sent back to Washington, DC, after he was found unconscious outside his hotel room in The Hague, Netherlands, while on official travel. When interviewed, the agent said he went out to dinner at a restaurant with other Secret Service personnel, during which he had several drinks. After dinner, he and two other agents had several more drinks. The agent could not remember leaving the restaurant or how he got back to his hotel. All three agents were found to have violated the 10-hour rule regarding alcohol consumption. The agent who was found unconscious resigned from the Secret Service. The other two agents were issued suspensions of 28 days and 30 days.
- In June 2014, a UD officer flying while armed with his Secret Service-issued handgun consumed 2 beers within the 10 hours prior to his flight. He consumed 1 beer at the airport bar after checking in with the gate agent as an armed law enforcement officer. He was issued a 14-day suspension.

REVIEW OF SYSTEMIC EMPLOYEE MISCONDUCT ISSUES

Although after the Cartagena incident, the Secret Service investigated the allegations of misconduct, took action against the employees involved, and issued new guidance on personal behavior, other underlying issues arose during our investigation. In particular, when asked how the Secret Service dealt with misconduct allegations in general, some employees alleged there was a culture of retaliation and disparate treatment of employees, including directed punishment toward complainants and those voicing concerns about Secret Service programs and operations. Secret Service staff reported that the resulting culture may have adversely impacted the employee retention rate. Individuals we interviewed also reported that Secret Service officials "whitewashed" allegations of employee misconduct, effectively downplaying and underreporting complaints to the Office of Inspector General (OIG) so they would appear to be administrative and not potentially criminal. These actions would, in turn, cause the allegations to be returned to Secret Service internal affairs for inquiry instead of OIG accepting them for investigation.

We decided to further examine these more general allegations, which pointed to potentially more wide-spread problems. In December 2013, we issued a report on our review of the Secret Service's efforts to identify, mitigate, and address instances of misconduct and inappropriate behavior. In our report, we described a situation in which many employees were hesitant to report off-duty misconduct either because of fear that they would be retaliated against or because they felt management would do nothing about it. For example, in response to one survey question, 56 percent of electronic survey respondents indicated that they could report misconduct without fear of retaliation, meaning that almost half of the workforce may have feared retaliation for reporting misconduct.

In our survey, we also questioned employees about reporting excessive alcohol consumption. Of the 138 electronic survey respondents who personally observed excessive alcohol consumption, 118 (86 percent) indicated they did not report the behavior. Respondents could select multiple reasons for not reporting the behavior. Some frequently cited reasons included:

- 66 respondents (56 percent) indicated the employee engaged in the behavior while off-duty.
- 55 respondents (47 percent) did not believe that management supported employees reporting the behavior.
- 47 respondents (40 percent) were afraid of reprisal or retaliation.

Additionally, we reported that the Secret Service often administered penalties that were less severe than the range of recommended penalties at other Department law enforcement components. We compared the Secret Service's disciplinary response for specific infractions to penalties for similar infractions at U.S. Immigration and Customs Enforcement (ICE), the Transportation Security Administration (TSA), and U.S. Customs and Border Patrol (CBP).

From 2004 to 2013, the Secret Service administered discipline for a single offense to one-time offenders 341 times. Most of the time, the Secret Service imposed less severe penalties than one or more of these components. Specifically:

- In 265 of the 341 instances (78 percent), the Secret Service administered less severe discipline than one or more of TSA's, ICE's, and CBP's tables of penalties showed those components would have administered. In 141 of these 265 instances (53 percent), the Secret Service administered less severe discipline compared to all three components' tables of penalties.
- For the remaining 76 of the 341 instances (22 percent), the Secret Service administered discipline within or above what TSA's, ICE's, and CBP's tables of penalties showed those components would have administered.

As a result of our findings, we identified areas in which the Secret Service needed better management controls for reporting misconduct or inappropriate behavior and adjudicating and administering disciplinary actions. We made 14 recommendations to improve the Secret Service's processes for identifying, mitigating, and addressing instances of misconduct and inappropriate behavior. Additionally, we suggested the Secret Service continue to monitor and address excessive alcohol consumption and personal conduct within its workforce.

The Secret Service concurred with all 14 recommendations and implemented changes to its discipline program. Among the improvements, the Secret Service created a table of penalties for determining appropriate corrective, disciplinary, or adverse actions for common offenses and established a centralized process within headquarters for determining and implementing discipline for employee misconduct. Because the Secret Service reformed its administrative discipline process after our report was issued, we are unable to determine the extent to which the pattern of imposing less severe discipline continues.

Correcting underlying shortcomings in the discipline process and ensuring fair and consistent discipline are vital to the stability of any organization. As part of our performance plan for fiscal year 2016, we intend to evaluate the strength of the Department's disciplinary processes. We will focus on the depth and breadth of employees' perceptions and attitudes about misconduct and the application of discipline, DHS's established rules of conduct, and the application of discipline across the Department.

OTHER AUDIT AND INSPECTION WORK INVOLVING SECRET SERVICE PROGRAMS AND OPERATIONS

We have also conducted several audit and inspection reports regarding Secret Service programmatic responsibilities, outside the area of employee misconduct.

Management Alert on UD Officer Fatigue

We recently issued a management alert in which we identified UD officer safety issues that impact officer safety and the Secret Service's ability to meet its mission.

Specifically, during a site visit for an unrelated audit, we observed two UD officers sleeping at their posts. Fatigue from travel, overtime shifts, and long hours contributed to these incidents. The Secret Service referred both officers for disciplinary action. We brought this matter to the attention of the Secret Service because of our concern that the staffing and scheduling process does not ensure officers have adequate breaks while on duty and time off between shifts. The Protective Mission Panel report, produced after the fence-jumping incident, raised concerns that the UD was inadequately staffed, necessitating significant overtime. We are concerned that the situation has not improved since that report was issued in December 2014.

Inoperable Alarm at Protectee's Residence

In October 2014, we visited former President George H.W. Bush's Houston residence in response to a complaint alleging alarms were inoperable. During our visit, we identified issues with the alarm system at the residence.

Specifically, an alarm, which had been installed around 1993, had been inoperable for at least 13 months. During this time, the Secret Service created a roving post to secure the residence, but the Secret Service could not determine the exact time period between when the alarm failed and the roving patrol started. We did not identify any security breaches that occurred. However, we found problems with identifying, reporting, and tracking alarm system malfunctions, and with repairing and replacing alarm systems. Secret Service officials also told us about security equipment problems, including the need for substantial repairs and improvements, at other residences of former Presidents.

FUTURE OIG WORK RELATED TO THE SECRET SERVICE

In addition to the work we have already completed, we intend to conduct audits or evaluations of a number of other Secret Service programs and operations:

- *On-going Reviews of Three Security Lapses.*—We are reviewing three incidents, one from November 2011 and two more that took place in September 2014, all of which highlight security lapses that raise serious concerns about the Secret Service's ability to accomplish its protective mission. For each incident—shots being fired at the White House from Constitution Avenue in November 2011, an intruder jumping over the fence and entering the White House in September 2014, and an armed guard coming in close proximity to the President in September 2014—we are determining whether the Secret Service followed its own protective policies, what actions were taken to correct identified deficiencies, and whether these corrections were adequate. The ultimate aim of our reviews is to determine and understand the root causes of these lapses, which may point to more fundamental and on-going challenges to the Secret Service's mission. This fiscal year, we plan to issue three reports on these incidents, as well as a capping report that identifies root causes and includes any other necessary, overarching recommendations.
- *Radio Communications.*—We are completing an audit to determine the adequacy of Secret Service radio communications. We will be recommending that the Secret Service upgrade its existing radio communication systems and develop a strategy and time line to continuously upgrade radio communication systems.
- *Protective Mission Panel Recommendations.*—This fiscal year, we plan to assess the implementation status of recommendations from the Protective Mission Panel to the Secret Service resulting from the September 2014 fence jumping incident.
- *Security Clearances.*—In response to a Congressional request, we will examine the Secret Service's practices of hiring and deploying personnel without completing the security clearance process. Specifically, we will review the process of granting waivers for personnel to begin work without completing the security clearance process, and the safeguards the Secret Service uses to ensure that those personnel are not given access to Classified information during the course of their duties.
- *IT Integration and Transformation.*—We will conduct an audit to determine the extent to which the Secret Service's IT Integration and Transformation (IITT) effort to modernize it outdated IT infrastructure supports its investigative and protective missions, goals, and objectives. Historically, the IITT has faced challenges in planning, staffing, and governance. In 2009, the DHS chief information officer determined the effort lacked adequate planning, the development schedule was too aggressive, and the program scope exceeded the allocated budget. As a result of a prior OIG audit, in March 2011, we recommended that the Secret Service develop an IT staffing plan, formalize its Executive Steering Committee, and provide the Secret Service Chief Information Officer with the component-wide IT budget and investment review authority needed to ensure success of the IITT. Since our prior audit, the Secret Service has reduced the scope of the IITT and is working with the DHS Chief Financial Officer to ensure that planned capabilities can be delivered within expected funding levels. We expect to complete our audit and issue a final report in the summer of 2016.

Mr. Chairmen, this concludes my prepared statement. I welcome any questions you or other Members of the subcommittees may have.

Mr. PERRY. Thank you, Mr. Roth.

The Chair now recognizes Mr. Willemssen for an opening statement.

STATEMENT OF JOEL C. WILLEMSSEN, MANAGING DIRECTOR, INFORMATION TECHNOLOGY ISSUES, U.S. GOVERNMENT ACCOUNTABILITY OFFICE

Mr. WILLEMSSEN. Thank you Chairman Perry, Chairman Lankford, Ranking Member Watson Coleman, Ranking Member Heitkamp, Chairman Johnson of the full committee, Ranking Member Thompson of the full committee, Members of the subcommittees, thank you for inviting GAO to testify today.

As requested, I will briefly summarize our statement on information security across the Federal Government. GAO has had long-standing concerns about the state of information security in the Federal Government. We initially identified Federal information security as a Government-wide high-risk area 18 years ago.

We subsequently expanded this high-risk designation to include computerized systems supporting the Nation's critical infrastructure and the protection of privacy and personally identifiable information. The cyber threats facing our country continue to be very serious.

The impact of these threats is highlighted by recent incidents involving breaches of sensitive, personally identifiable information and the sharp increase in information security incidents reported by Federal agencies over the last several years, which have risen from about 5,500 in 2006 to about 67,000 in 2014.

Given the risks posed by external and internal threats in the increasing number of incidents, it is crucial that Federal agencies take appropriate steps to secure their systems and data. However, we and inspectors general have continued to identify significant weaknesses and needed security controls.

For example for fiscal year 2014, 19 of 24 major Federal agencies declared information security as a material weakness or significant deficiency. Most of these agencies have reported weaknesses in the key control areas that we track, including controls intended to prevent, limit, or detect unauthorized or inappropriate access to networks and data. In particular, our work has often shown that too many agency employees have too much unnecessary access to too many systems and databases.

Agencies need to implement clear policies on access to sensitive information and grant access permissions to users at the minimum level necessary to perform legitimate job-related tasks on a need-to-know basis. Deploying effective monitoring and accountability mechanisms to track user activities on networks and systems is also essential to ensuring that improper access and usage are quickly detected and remedied.

To address the many information security weaknesses at Federal agencies, GAO and inspectors general have made thousands of recommendations. Over the last 6 years, GAO has made about 2,000 recommendations to improve information security programs and controls.

To date about 58 percent of these recommendations have been implemented. Until agencies take actions to address weakness and implement GAO and I.G. recommendations, Federal networks and sensitive information, including personally identifiable information, will be at increased risk from internal and external threats.

Actions to implement recommendations will strengthen systems and data security and reduce the risk of cyber intrusions or attacks. That concludes the summary my statement and I look forward to addressing the questions.

Thank you.

[The prepared statement of Mr. Willemssen follows:]

PREPARED STATEMENT OF JOEL C. WILLEMSSEN

NOVEMBER 17, 2015

Chairman Lankford, Chairman Perry, Ranking Members Heitkamp and Watson Coleman, and Members of the subcommittees: Thank you for inviting me to testify at today's hearing on on-going challenges at the U.S. Secret Service and their Government-wide implications. As requested, my statement today will address cyber threats and security control weaknesses affecting Federal systems and information.

As you know, the Federal Government faces an evolving array of cyber-based threats to its systems and data, as illustrated by recently-reported data breaches at Federal agencies, which have affected millions of current and former Federal employees, and the increasing number of incidents reported by agencies. Such incidents underscore the urgent need for effective implementation of information security controls at Federal agencies.

Since 1997, we have designated Federal information security as a Government-wide high-risk area, and in 2003 expanded this area to include computerized systems supporting the Nation's critical infrastructure. Most recently, in the February 2015 update to our high-risk list, we further expanded this area to include protecting the privacy of personally identifiable information (PII)[1]—that is, personal information that is collected, maintained, and shared by both Federal and non-Federal entities.[2]

In preparing this statement, we relied on our previous work addressing cyber threats and Federal information security efforts. The prior reports cited throughout this statement contain detailed discussions of the scope of the work and the methodology used to carry it out. All the work on which this statement is based was conducted in accordance with generally-accepted Government auditing standards. Those standards require that we plan and perform audits to obtain sufficient, appropriate evidence to provide a reasonable basis for our findings and conclusions based on our audit objectives. We believe that the evidence obtained provides a reasonable basis for our findings and conclusions based on our audit objectives. A list of related GAO products is provided in attachment I.

BACKGROUND

As computer technology has advanced, the Federal Government has become increasingly dependent on computerized information systems to carry out operations and to process, maintain, and report essential information. Federal agencies rely on computer systems to transmit proprietary and other sensitive information, develop and maintain intellectual capital, conduct operations, process business transactions, transfer funds, and deliver services.

Ineffective protection of these information systems and networks can impair delivery of vital services, and result in:
- loss or theft of computer resources, assets, and funds;
- inappropriate access to and disclosure, modification, or destruction of sensitive information, such as personally identifiable information;
- disruption of essential operations supporting critical infrastructure, National defense, or emergency services;
- undermining of agency missions due to embarrassing incidents that erode the public's confidence in Government;
- use of computer resources for unauthorized purposes or to launch attacks on other systems;
- damage to networks and equipment; and
- high costs for remediation.

Recognizing the importance of these issues, Congress enacted laws intended to improve the protection of Federal information and systems. These laws include the *Federal Information Security Modernization Act of 2014* (FISMA),[3] which, among other things, authorizes the Department of Homeland Security (DHS) to: (1) Assist the Office of Management and Budget (OMB) with overseeing and monitoring agencies' implementation of security requirements; (2) operate the Federal information

---

[1] Personally identifiable information is information about an individual, including information that can be used to distinguish or trace an individual's identity, such as name, Social Security number, mother's maiden name, or biometric records, and any other personal information that is linked or linkable to an individual.

[2] See GAO, *High-Risk Series: An Update*, GAO 15-290 (Washington, DC: Feb. 11, 2015).

[3] The *Federal Information Security Modernization Act of 2014* (Pub. L. No. 113-283, Dec. 18, 2014) (2014 FISMA) largely superseded the very similar *Federal Information Security Management Act of 2002* (Title III, Pub. L. No. 107-347, Dec. 17, 2002) (2002 FISMA).

security incident center; and (3) provide agencies with operational and technical assistance, such as that for continuously diagnosing and mitigating cyber threats and vulnerabilities. The act also reiterated the 2002 FISMA requirement for the head of each agency to provide information security protections commensurate with the risk and magnitude of the harm resulting from unauthorized access, use, disclosure, disruption, modification, or destruction of the agency's information or information systems.

In addition, the act continues the requirement for Federal agencies to develop, document, and implement an agency-wide information security program. The program is to provide security for the information and information systems that support the operations and assets of the agency, including those provided or managed by another agency, contractor, or other source.

CYBER THREATS TO FEDERAL SYSTEMS CONTINUE TO EVOLVE AMID INCREASING NUMBERS OF INCIDENTS

Risks to cyber-based assets can originate from unintentional or intentional threats. Unintentional threats can be caused by, among other things, natural disasters, defective computer or network equipment, software coding errors, and the actions of careless or poorly-trained employees. Intentional threats include both targeted and untargeted attacks from a variety of sources, including criminal groups, hackers, disgruntled employees and other organizational insiders, foreign nations engaged in espionage and information warfare, and terrorists.

These adversaries vary in terms of their capabilities, willingness to act, and motives, which can include seeking monetary or personal gain or pursuing a political, economic, or military advantage. For example, organizational insiders can pose threats to an organization since their position within the organization often allows them to gain unrestricted access and cause damage to the targeted system, steal system data, or disclose sensitive information without authorization. The insider threat includes inappropriate actions by contractors hired by the organization, as well as careless or poorly-trained employees.

As we reported in February 2015,[4] since fiscal year 2006, the number of information security incidents affecting systems supporting the Federal Government has steadily increased each year: Rising from 5,503 in fiscal year 2006 to 67,168 in fiscal year 2014, an increase of 1,121 percent. Furthermore, the number of reported security incidents involving PII at Federal agencies has more than doubled in recent years—from 10,481 incidents in fiscal year 2009 to 27,624 incidents in fiscal year 2014. (See fig 1.)

---

[4] GAO, *High-Risk Series: An Update*, GAO–15–290 (Washington, DC: February 2015).

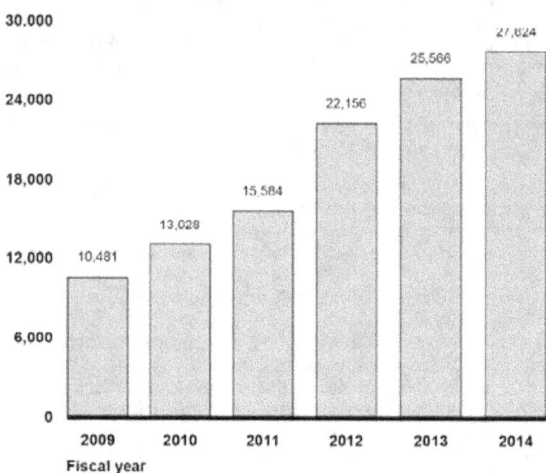

Figure 1: Incidents Involving Personally Identifiable Information Reported to the U.S. Computer Emergency Readiness Team by Federal Agencies for Fiscal Years 2009 through 2014

Number of reported incidents

Source: GAO analysis of United States Computer Emergency Readiness Team data for fiscal years 2009-2014. | GAO-16-194T

These incidents and others like them can adversely affect National security; damage public health and safety; and lead to inappropriate access to and disclosure, modification, or destruction of sensitive information. Recent examples highlight the impact of such incidents:

- In June 2015, the Office of Personnel Management reported that an intrusion into its systems affected the personnel records of about 4.2 million current and former Federal employees. The Director stated that a separate but related incident involved the agency's background investigation systems and compromised background investigation files for 21.5 million individuals.
- In June 2015, the Commissioner of the Internal Revenue Service testified that unauthorized third parties had gained access to taxpayer information from its "Get Transcript" application. According to officials, criminals used taxpayer-specific data acquired from non-Department sources to gain unauthorized access to information on approximately 100,000 tax accounts. This data included Social Security information, dates of birth, and street addresses. In an August 2015 update, the agency reported this number to be about 114,000 and that an additional 220,000 accounts had been inappropriately accessed, which brings the total to about 330,000 accounts.
- In April 2015, the Department of Veterans Affairs' Office of Inspector General reported that two contractors had improperly accessed the agency's network from foreign countries using personally-owned equipment.[5]
- In February 2015, the director of national intelligence stated that unauthorized computer intrusions were detected in 2014 on the networks of the Office of Personnel Management and two of its contractors. The two contractors were involved in processing sensitive PII related to National security clearances for Federal employees.[6]

---

[5] Department of Veterans Affairs, Office of Inspector General, *Administrative Investigation Improper Access to the VA Network by VA Contractors from Foreign Countries Office of Information and Technology Austin, TX, Report No. 10–01730–159 (Washington, DC: April 2015).*

[6] James R. Clapper, Director of National Intelligence, *World-wide Threat Assessment of the U.S. Intelligence Community*, testimony before the Senate Committee on Armed Services, February 26, 2015.

- In September 2014, a cyber intrusion into the United States Postal Service's information systems may have compromised PII for more than 800,000 of its employees.[7]
- In October 2013, a wide-scale cybersecurity breach involving a U.S. Food and Drug Administration system occurred that exposed the PII of 14,000 user accounts.[8]

INFORMATION SECURITY WEAKNESSES PLACE FEDERAL SYSTEMS AND SENSITIVE DATA AT RISK

Given the risks posed by cyber threats and the increasing number of incidents, it is crucial that Federal agencies take appropriate steps to secure their systems and information. We and agency inspectors general have identified numerous weaknesses in protecting Federal information and systems. Agencies continue to have shortcomings in assessing risks, developing and implementing security controls, and monitoring results. Specifically, for fiscal year 2014, 19 of the 24 Federal agencies covered by the *Chief Financial Officers Act*[9] reported that information security control deficiencies were either a material weakness or a significant deficiency in internal controls over their financial reporting.[10] Moreover, inspectors general at 23 of the 24 agencies cited information security as a major management challenge for their agency.

As we reported in September 2015, for fiscal year 2014, most of the 24 agencies had weaknesses in the 5 major categories of information system controls.[11] These control categories are: (1) Access controls, which limit or detect access to computer resources (data, programs, equipment, and facilities), thereby protecting them against unauthorized modification, loss, and disclosure; (2) configuration management controls, intended to prevent unauthorized changes to information system resources (for example, software programs and hardware configurations) and assure that software is current and known vulnerabilities are patched; (3) segregation of duties, which prevents a single individual from controlling all critical stages of a process by splitting responsibilities between 2 or more organizational groups; (4) contingency planning,[12] which helps avoid significant disruptions in computer-dependent operations; and (5) agency-wide security management, which provides a framework for ensuring that risks are understood and that effective controls are selected, implemented, and operating as intended. (See fig. 2.)

---

[7] Randy S. Miskanic, Secure Digital Solutions Vice President of the United States Postal Service, *Examining Data Security at the United States Postal Service*, testimony before the Subcommittee on Federal Workforce, U.S. Postal Service and the Census, 113th Congress, November 19, 2014.

[8] Department of Health and Human Services, Office of Inspector General, *Penetration Test of the Food and Drug Administration's Computer Network*, Report No. A–18–13–30331 (Washington, DC: October 2014).

[9] The 24 agencies are the Departments of Agriculture, Commerce, Defense, Education, Energy, Health and Human Services, Homeland Security, Housing and Urban Development, the Interior, Justice, Labor, State, Transportation, the Treasury, and Veterans Affairs; the Environmental Protection Agency; General Services Administration; National Aeronautics and Space Administration; National Science Foundation; Nuclear Regulatory Commission; Office of Personnel Management; Small Business Administration; Social Security Administration; and the U.S. Agency for International Development.

[10] A material weakness is a deficiency, or combination of deficiencies, that results in more than a remote likelihood that a material misstatement of the financial statements will not be prevented or detected. A significant deficiency is a control deficiency, or combination of control deficiencies, in internal control that is less severe than a material weakness, yet important enough to merit attention by those charged with governance. A control deficiency exists when the design or operation of a control does not allow management or employees, in the normal course of performing their assigned functions, to prevent or detect and correct misstatements on a timely basis.

[11] GAO, *Federal Information Security: Agencies Need to Correct Weaknesses and Fully Implement Security Programs*, GAO–15–714 (Washington, DC: Sept. 29, 2015).

[12] Contingency planning for information systems is part of an overall organizational program for achieving continuity of operations for mission/business operations.

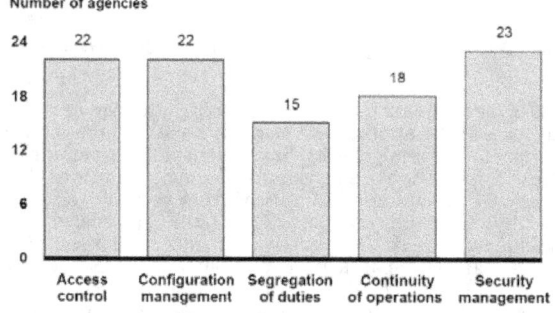

Figure 2: Information Security Weaknesses at 24 Federal Agencies for Fiscal Year 2014

Number of agencies

Source: GAO analysis of agency, inspector general, and GAO reports as of May 2015. | GAO-16-194T

- *Access controls.*—For fiscal year 2014, we, agencies, and inspectors general reported weaknesses in the electronic and physical controls to limit, prevent, or detect inappropriate access to computer resources (data, equipment, and facilities), thereby increasing their risk of unauthorized use, modification, disclosure, and loss. Access controls involve the 6 critical elements described in table 1.

TABLE 1.—CRITICAL ELEMENTS FOR ACCESS CONTROL TO COMPUTER RESOURCES

Element	Description
Boundary Protection	Boundary protection controls logical connectivity into and out of networks and controls connectivity to and from devices that are connected to a network. For example, multiple firewalls can be deployed to prevent both outsiders and trusted insiders from gaining unauthorized access to systems, and intrusion detection and prevention technologies can be deployed to defend against attacks from the internet.
User Identification and Authentication.	A computer system must be able to identify and authenticate different users so that activities on the system can be linked to specific individuals. When an organization assigns a unique user account to specific users, the system is able to distinguish one user from another—a process called identification. The system also must establish the validity of a user's claimed identity by requesting some kind of information, such as a password, that is known only by the user—a process known as authentication. Multifactor authentication involves using two or more factors to achieve authentication. Factors include something you know (password or personal identification number), something you have (cryptographic identification device or token), or something you are (biometric). The combination of identification and authentication provides the basis for establishing accountability and for controlling access to the system.

TABLE 1.—CRITICAL ELEMENTS FOR ACCESS CONTROL TO COMPUTER RESOURCES—Continued

Element	Description
Authorization	Authorization is the process of granting or denying access rights and permissions to a protected resource, such as a network, a system, an application, a function, or a file. For example, operating systems have some built-in authorization features such as permissions for files and folders. Network devices, such as routers, may have access control lists that can be used to authorize users who can access and perform certain actions on the device. Authorization controls help implement the principle of "least privilege," which the National Institute of Standards and Technology describes as allowing only authorized accesses for users (or processes acting on behalf of users) which are necessary to accomplish assigned tasks in accordance with organizational missions and business functions.
Cryptography	Cryptography underlies many of the mechanisms used to enforce the confidentiality and integrity of critical and sensitive information. Examples of cryptographic services are encryption, authentication, digital signature, and key management. Cryptographic tools help control access to information by making it unintelligible to unauthorized users and by protecting the integrity of transmitted or stored information.
Auditing and Monitoring	To establish individual accountability, monitor compliance with security policies, and investigate security violations, it is necessary to determine what, when, and by whom specific actions have been taken on a system. Agencies do so by implementing software that provides an audit trail, or logs of system activity, that they can use to determine the source of a transaction or attempted transaction and to monitor users' activities.
Physical Security	Physical security controls help protect computer facilities and resources from espionage, sabotage, damage, and theft. Examples of physical security controls include perimeter fencing, surveillance cameras, security guards, locks, and procedures for granting or denying individuals physical access to computing resources. Physical controls also include environmental controls such as smoke detectors, fire alarms, extinguishers, and uninterruptible power supplies. Considerations for perimeter security include controlling vehicular and pedestrian traffic. In addition, visitors' access to sensitive areas is to be managed appropriately.

Source: GAO. GAO–16–194T

For fiscal year 2014, 12 agencies had weaknesses reported in protecting their networks and system boundaries. For example, the access control lists on one agency's firewall did not prevent traffic coming or initiated from the public internet protocol addresses of a contractor site and a U.S. telecom corporation from entering its network. Additionally, 20 agencies, including DHS, had weaknesses reported in their ability to appropriately identify and authenticate system users. To illustrate, agencies had weak password controls, such as using system passwords that had not been changed from the easily guessable default passwords or did not expire.

Eighteen agencies, including DHS, had weaknesses reported in authorization controls for fiscal year 2014. For example, one agency had not consistently or in a timely manner removed, transferred, and/or terminated employee and contractor access privileges from multiple systems. Another agency also had granted access privileges unnecessarily, which sometimes allowed users of an internal network to read and write files containing sensitive system information. In fiscal year 2014, 4 agencies had weaknesses reported in the use of encryption for protecting data.

In addition, DHS and 18 other agencies had weaknesses reported in implementing an effective audit and monitoring capability. For instance, one agency did not sufficiently log security-relevant events on the servers and network devices of a key system. Moreover, 10 agencies, including DHS, had weaknesses reported in their ability to restrict physical access or harm to computer resources and protect them from unauthorized loss or impairment. For example, a contractor of an agency was granted physical access to a server room without the required approval of the office director.

- *Configuration management.*—For fiscal year 2014, 22 agencies, including DHS, had weaknesses reported in controls that are intended to ensure that only authorized and fully-tested software is placed in operation, software and hardware is updated, information systems are monitored, patches are applied to these systems to protect against known vulnerabilities, and emergency changes are documented and approved. For example, 17 agencies, including DHS, had weaknesses reported with installing software patches and implementing current versions of software in a timely manner.
- *Segregation of duties.*—Fifteen agencies, including DHS, had weaknesses in controls for segregation of duties. These controls are the policies, procedures, and organizational structure that help to ensure that one individual cannot independently control all key aspects of a computer-related operation and thereby take unauthorized actions or gain unauthorized access to assets or records. For example, a developer from one agency had been authorized inappropriate access to the production environment of the agency's system.
- *Continuity of operations.*—DHS and 17 other agencies had weaknesses reported in controls for their continuity of operations practices for fiscal year 2014. Specifically, 16 agencies did not have a comprehensive contingency plan. For example, one agency's contingency plans had not been updated to reflect changes in the system boundaries, roles, and responsibilities, and lessons learned from testing contingency plans at alternate processing and storage sites. Additionally, 15 agencies had not regularly tested their contingency plans.
- *Security management.*—For fiscal year 2014, DHS and 22 other agencies had weaknesses reported in security management, which is an underlying cause for information security weaknesses identified at Federal agencies. An agency-wide security program, as required by FISMA, provides a framework for assessing and managing risk, including developing and implementing security policies and procedures, conducting security awareness training, monitoring the adequacy of the entity's computer-related controls through security tests and evaluations, and implementing remedial actions as appropriate.

We have also identified inconsistencies with the Government's approach to cybersecurity, including the following:

Overseeing the security controls of contractors providing IT services.—In August 2014, we reported that 5 of 6 agencies we reviewed were inconsistent in overseeing assessments of contractors' implementation of security controls.[13] This was partly because agencies had not documented IT security procedures for effectively overseeing contractor performance. In addition, according to OMB, 16 of 24 agency inspectors general determined that their agency's program for managing contractor systems lacked at least one required element.

Responding to cyber incidents.—In April 2014, we reported that the 24 agencies did not consistently demonstrate that they had effectively responded to cyber incidents.[14] Specifically, we estimated that agencies had not completely documented actions taken in response to detected incidents reported in fiscal year 2012 in about 65 percent of cases.[15] In addition, the 6 agencies we reviewed had not fully developed comprehensive policies, plans, and procedures to guide their incident response activities.

Responding to breaches of PII.—In December 2013, we reported that 8 Federal agencies had inconsistently implemented policies and procedures for responding to

---

[13] GAO, *Information Security: Agencies Need to Improve Oversight of Contractor Controls*, GAO–14–612 (Washington, DC: Aug. 8, 2014).

[14] GAO, *Information Security: Agencies Need to Improve Cyber Incident Response Practices*, GAO–14–354 (Washington, DC: Apr. 30, 2014).

[15] This estimate was based on a statistical sample of cyber incidents reported in fiscal year 2012, with 95 percent confidence that the estimate falls between 58 and 72 percent.

data breaches involving PII.[16] In addition, OMB requirements for reporting PII-related data breaches were not always feasible or necessary. Thus, we concluded that agencies may not be consistently taking actions to limit the risk to individuals from PII-related data breaches and may be expending resources to meet OMB reporting requirements that provide little value.

Over the last several years, we and agency inspectors general have made thousands of recommendations to agencies aimed at improving their implementation of information security controls. For example, we have made about 2,000 recommendations over the last 6 years. These recommendations identify actions for agencies to take in protecting their information and systems. To illustrate, we and inspectors general have made recommendations for agencies to correct weaknesses in controls intended to prevent, limit, and detect unauthorized access to computer resources, such as controls for protecting system boundaries, identifying and authenticating users, authorizing users to access systems, encrypting sensitive data, and auditing and monitoring activity on their systems. We have also made recommendations for agencies to implement their information security programs and protect the privacy of PII held on their systems.

However, many agencies continue to have weaknesses in implementing these controls in part because many of these recommendations remain unimplemented. For example, about 42 percent of the recommendations we have made during the last 6 years remain unimplemented. Until Federal agencies take actions to implement the recommendations made by us and the inspectors general—Federal systems and information, as well as sensitive personal information about the public, will be at an increased risk of compromise from cyber-based attacks and other threats.

In conclusion, the dangers posed by a wide array of cyber threats facing the Nation are heightened by weaknesses in the Federal Government's approach to protecting its systems and information. While recent Government-wide initiatives, including the 30-day Cybersecurity Sprint,[17] hold promise for bolstering the Federal cybersecurity posture, it is important to note that no single technology or set of practices is sufficient to protect against all these threats. A "defense in depth" strategy that includes well-trained personnel, effective and consistently applied processes, and appropriately implemented technologies is required. While agencies have elements of such a strategy in place, more needs to be done to fully implement it and to address existing weaknesses. In particular, implementing our and agency inspectors general recommendations will strengthen agencies' ability to protect their systems and information, reducing the risk of a potentially devastating cyber attack.

Chairman Lankford, Chairman Perry, Ranking Members Heitkamp and Watson Coleman, and Members of the subcommittees, this concludes my statement. I would be happy to answer your questions.

Mr. PERRY. Thank you Mr. Willemssen. Chair now recognizes himself for some questions beginning with Mr. Roth.

Mr. Roth, how many subpoenas regarding the Chaffetz incident and the MCI, the Master Central Index, how many subpoenas were issued?

Mr. ROTH. I believe it was only one subpoena.

Mr. PERRY. So why if there were multiple individuals that admittedly breached the information and may have compromised it why would only one subpoena be issued? Why wouldn't there be multiple subpoenas issued for multiple individuals?

Mr. ROTH. Well, most of the information that we received were from Government data systems so no subpoena would be necessary. The only time we have to subpoena information is if we were going to a third party, like a telephone record provider for example.

Typically it is our policy in these kinds of circumstances to have a level of predication before we go and subpoena somebody's personal telephone records. We had predication only on one individual

---

[16] GAO, *Information Security: Agency Responses to Breaches of Personally Identifiable Information Need to Be More Consistent*, GAO–14–34 (Washington, DC: Dec. 9, 2013).

[17] In June 2015, the Federal Chief Information Officer launched the 30-day Cybersecurity Sprint, during which agencies were to take immediate actions to combat cyber threats within 30 days. Actions included patching critical vulnerabilities, tightening policies and practices for privileged users, and accelerating the implementation of multifactor authentication.

rather than the hundreds who may have had access to that information.

Mr. PERRY. Even those who admitted to wrongdoing?

Mr. ROTH. That is correct.

Mr. PERRY. Was the Index searched for other improper access incidences?

Mr. ROTH. It was not. The Index itself was created in 1984. It did not have the ability to readily do the kinds of forensics that you would do on a modern data system. In fact, what we were required to do, that is what the administrators of the database were required to do, were actually write scripts or programs to be able to find access to this information.

It was a highly time-consuming kind of a thing and because the—sort of the necessity for finding answers as quickly as we could, we only restricted it to Chairman Chaffetz's name.

Mr. PERRY. So then, based on that, would it be correct to say that we have absolutely no idea at this point regarding that data system, the Master Central Index, if any other Americans or any other citizens have had similar things occur regarding their personally identifiable information, whether it was searched, whether it was divulged. We have no idea?

Mr. ROTH. That is correct.

Mr. PERRY. That is a bit unsettling. Director Clancy, are you familiar with Operation Moonlight?

Mr. CLANCY. Sir, I am familiar with some of the details of that, yes.

Mr. PERRY. Can you just inform us? I understand you have got thousand of employees. This hearing is not meant to impugn or besmirch the credibility of your agency. I think Americans have traditionally and currently, have the highest regard and want to have that. But how does that—something like that happen? Can you?

Mr. CLANCY. Yes sir.

Mr. PERRY. So Secret Service agents used Government information, accessed databases and then used equipment, time, material to surveil essentially, a private citizen's property without any due cause of anything. Is that essentially—I mean, that is my narrative but what is yours? Then how does that happen?

Mr. CLANCY. Sir forgive me as I was not here during that time frame so I am going to rely on some briefings when I first came in as the acting director and it was found as the OIG's report illustrates, people made very poor decisions. There was misjudgment. It should not have happened and there were some changes made in our management.

Mr. PERRY. Well, I will tell you. I looked at—and I imagine you are familiar with it. I am just going to read you the subject, is "Directive 2015–09, Disciplinary and Adverse Actions". Right?

Mr. CLANCY. Yes sir.

Mr. PERRY. It is from your agency and I guess it is moving forward based on what has occurred regarding the information in the data breach. I just wanted to give you a flavor of what I see here: "An employee is entitled to," "the employee is entitled to," "the employee is entitled to"—I am just kind of going through each paragraph——

"The employee will be provided with;" "the employee shall have an opportunity to;" "the employee is entitled to". You kind-of get my gist, and the reason I say that is—what I am wondering is and I think what a lot of Americans wondering is what are the consequences of the actions of 45 or 41 employees who accessed Mr. Chaffetz's data and then whoever disseminated it up to 60 times?

What are the consequences to those individuals? We see what the employee's rights are.

Mr. CLANCY. Yes.

Mr. PERRY. Right?

Mr. CLANCY. Yes sir.

Mr. PERRY. But what are the consequences? How does Mr. Chaffetz get his reputation back? What is going to happen to these individuals? What is currently happening? Where do things stand?

Mr. CLANCY. Mr. Chairman, Secretary Johnson and I met and talked about this in a true sense of transparency because myself and my executive staff have been all interviewed in this case. We made a joint decision that the Department of Homeland Security would make the proposals. In this case I will tell you—and I have heard the comments that were made today, of reprehensible, disturbing, embarrassing.

I agree with everything that has been said here today and my workforce does as well. In fact, this hearing today will help me get this word out, the importance of protecting PII. We have all this, the training and we have the ethics guides and we go out and train are new recruits but a hearing like this puts a definitive stamp on our failures.

In this case, the individuals to answer your questions, Mr. Chairman, in this case, we are proposing, as of today, approximately 42—I don't—don't hold me to that number, approximately 42 will be issued a proposal of discipline ranging from anywhere from 3 days to 12 days of a suspension.

Mr. PERRY. So that is the maximum? The maximum is 12 days of—I am going to—the Chair is going to indulge himself on the time here a little bit. I am following a lot of questioning. So the maximum penalty, the maximum of repercussion for doing—we all know that when you look at these computer systems there is a warning in front that this is to be used for official business only and we all know.

Look, I hold as your folks do, a Secret security clearance, Top Secret security clearance. Everybody in the rooms knows, everybody in your agency knows that using this information for what it was used for was incorrect, improper, unauthorized, illegal.

The most we can hope for, the most disciplinary—toughest, disciplinary action right now is not a loss or revocation of your Secret security clearance, not the loss of your employment, it is 12 days suspension? I just want to be clear? Is that correct?

Mr. CLANCY. Mr. Chairman, that is for the Grades 15 and below. Those proposals have been issued as of today I am pretty sure on that. The SES-level folks have not had their discipline proposed as of this date.

Mr. PERRY. Is Mr. Lowery an SES-level employee?

Mr. CLANCY. He is, yes.

Mr. PERRY. What is the range of options of discipline or consequence for Mr. Lowery, if you can inform—I am not asking you to tell us which one it is because maybe you are still completing your investigation, but what can we expect?

Mr. CLANCY. The range goes from a letter of reprimand all the way up to removal.

Mr. PERRY. Thank you. The Chair now recognizes the gentleman from Oklahoma.

Senator LANKFORD. Would like to defer my questioning time to the Ranking Member. She has to be on the floor actually, of the Senate in a little bit. Actually working through a bill, so I would like to defer my time.

Mr. PERRY. So ordered.

Senator HEITKAMP. Thank you, Chairman Lankford.

Every one of the—Mr. Clancy—Director Clancy, every incident that we know of, there seems like there wasn't an adult in the room. That there was no one who provided that voice of saying, "Hey, guys, this is not the way to do this. Hey, we have a responsibility that is higher."

So while we look at management and we look at resources, you said in your testimony, you talked about how the corporate culture of the Secret Service is a priceless commodity.

Every day that priceless commodity gets threatened by agents not willing to be the adult in the room, not willing to be the person who stands up and says, knock it off. Because you can't do it just from a management standpoint. You have got to change the culture at the bottom and I think that is one of the concerns we have.

Is that it seems like all of this has happened with a great impunity and almost—you know, you can't touch me, you know, as the Chairman just talked about, or it is okay to do this. So, I want to know as we look at management changes, as we look at systemic rules and policies, those rules and policies are only as good as the commitment that people at every level within the Secret Service have for change.

So what are you doing within the Secret Service to build capacity for people to be the adult in the room, to stop this at the source and say this is not what we do in the Secret Service?

Mr. CLANCY. Thank you, Senator. This discipline system that we have in place now is relatively new. It is approximately 2 years old and then with—which includes a table of penalties. In the past, discipline was handled at a more local level. Now everything is funneled up to our Office of Integrity.

Senator HEITKAMP. I don't mean to interrupt but I am not talking about discipline. I am talking about culture and obviously consequences are part of changing that culture. But what about the integrity at every level? Of basically saying we don't do this. We don't go to hotels and hire, you know, people to service us.

We don't, you know, drive into the White House and disrupt a major investigation. We don't access a Congressman's secret records. We don't do that. Who is the person? How are we training people at every level to stand up and stop this behavior? Because I don't think we can do it just having hearings like this.

I think we have got to restore this priceless commodity that you are talking about, which is the integrity element of the men and women at every level, knowing that it is their responsibility to help maintain the integrity of the Secret Service.

Mr. CLANCY. I agree with you, Senator. We have to do more in terms of communicating with our people. We can have all the training exercises and all the on-line training, but for example, I have been to approximately 10 of our field offices, all of our protective details. I speak personally to our agents. I walk around the White House, talk to the officers.

I meet all the recruits prior to their graduation, both agent and UD. I tell them what they represent and what is expected of them. But I have got to do more of that as well as our staff. We have to just keep communicating, keep communicating to our people.

Again, what the Congress is doing today is a help to us and to our agency because again, the seriousness of what we have done in this particular case, resonates by these types of hearings.

Senator HEITKAMP. Thank you, Mr. Chairman. Yield back.

Mr. PERRY. The Chair thanks the gentlelady.

The Chair recognizes Mrs. Watson Coleman from New Jersey.

Mrs. WATSON COLEMAN. Thank you, Mr. Chairman.

Mr. Director, I want to talk about the Protective Mission Panel's recommendations. One of the things I think was noted in the panel was that we needed new leadership. We needed leadership from outside of this organization that didn't have the long-term relationships that might be somehow influenced by the relationships they did have and seeing it in a sort of insular way.

You have a 27-year record or experience with the agency. Clearly, you are an insider. There was a removal of a number of deputies and they were replaced. The majority of the deputies that were replaced were also from within the agency with long service records.

My question is: How do we change the culture of the organization if the very top leadership has been a part of that culture and perhaps only sees this organization from within?

Would we have not been better served had you identified the capacity to go to the outside and find people with certain skills, leadership abilities, accountabilities that would have transcended the relationships that individuals may have had?

Could that possibly have helped us to become more efficient, more effective, and more accountable as an agency?

Mr. CLANCY. Thank you for that question. I will tell you that I respect if you, if many, that thought that this position, the director's position, should have been someone from the outside. There is good reason for that. I understand that.

I consider the fact that I left the Service for 3 years, worked in private industry, has allowed me to bring in some outside views on how to run a business and how to run this agency. So what I did do is, first of all, I brought in a chief operating officer, a civilian from outside the agency.

That COO, chief operating officer, is equivalent to the deputy director. Additionally, we have created a lot of subject-matter expert positions where traditionally, they answer to agents—you know, prior to me arriving here, all of the top-level security was run by agents. Some of them, candidly, were not subject-matter experts.

For example, finance. We now have a chief financial officer who does not answer directly to an assistant director who is an agent, she is the chief financial officer. Chief technology officer is an engineer, not an agent. The chief strategy officer is a lawyer who is not an agent. There are a few others as well.

So we have brought in, we are trying to bring in this outside perspective to run this business but also move the agents into our core mission of protection and investigations.

Mrs. WATSON COLEMAN. So talk to me a little bit about your ability to bring in not only new people into the agency, but more diverse people. Because the information that I have read regarding the Secret Service is that it is predominantly white male.

There is a small percentage of women and not very—not consistent with across the board in Federal Government. What are you doing to address the issue of lack of diversity in terms of race and ethnicity and gender in positions? What are you doing to address the long-standing and outstanding issue with the civil rights complaints?

Mr. CLANCY. Yes.

Mrs. WATSON COLEMAN. Moving beyond them as opposed to using the system to delay the implementation of the corrective actions that could be taking place. Thank you.

Mr. CLANCY. In terms of diversity, I think I would ask you first to look at my executive staff. On that staff of approximately 12 people, we have 5 African-Americans, 6 females. But going down throughout the ranks, you are correct. We are not where we want to be with diversity.

So we are targeting universities that provide diversity for us. We have shortened our hiring process where we can go to these universities and over a weekend period of time, do a testing, an interview and a polygraph if the first two steps are met.

But we are targeting specific areas of the country to really work on this diversity because we are deficient in that area, certainly with females as well. We are working diligently to try to improve that diversity.

Mrs. WATSON COLEMAN. Thank you. I yield back for another.

Mr. PERRY. Chair thanks the gentlelady. The Chair now recognizes Mr. Johnson from Wisconsin.

Senator JOHNSON. Thank you, Mr. Chairman. Inspector General Roth, in your written testimony, you state that, "Information was accessed by Secret Service employees on approximately 60 occasions between March 25 and April 2nd of this year." Then you went on to say, "We concluded that a vast majority of those who accessed this information did so in violation of the Privacy Act of 1974."

What are the penalties for violating the Privacy Act of 1974?

Mr. ROTH. There are civil penalties for the agency that is involved if there is a wide-spread sort of gross negligence standard. So there are civil penalties, that is monetary penalties, for the agency involved. For individuals who accessed the system—improperly, knowing that it was protected under the Privacy Act that is a misdemeanor, which has a fine as a penalty but no custodial sentence.

Senator JOHNSON. Is there any Department of Justice investigation being undertaken right now to determine whether those misdemeanors were in fact going to—are they going to be prosecuted?

Mr. ROTH. No. During the course of our investigation we presented a case, the most compelling case we had and it was declined by the U.S. attorney's office.

Senator JOHNSON. Why would that be?

Mr. ROTH. There are several reasons. First of all, each individual agent has a Fifth Amendment right to not speak to us if in fact he is under criminal jeopardy. So we could not interview individuals, compel their interview, which we ultimately had to do in this case for a lack of voluntary cooperation.

So the level of evidence that the Department of Justice had was not sufficient for them to move forward. Additionally, when one looks at the penalty, it was simply a matter of competing resources.

Senator JOHNSON. Director Clancy, you know, I got involved in looking into the cultural problems with the Secret Service back in early 2012 after the events at Cartagena. This is not why I ran for the United States Senate, was to look into the Secret Service. It is an agency that we all want to have a high deal of credibility and note, as you stated in your testimony, the culture—in many respects is almost, you know, beyond reproach.

I mean, it is a fabulous agency, they are doing great work. But on the other hand, there is a real cultural problem. What are you going to do about it? I mean, I hear communication. I understand communication but actions speak far louder than words. When we are just talking a disciplinary process when there are violations of the Privacy Act and there are no prosecutions of it.

There is nobody held to—even the misdemeanor penalties. There is nothing more corrosive in an organization that has a cultural problem when misdeeds go unpunished. So what actions are going to be taken? This is 3 years now.

You know, Cartagena occurred in April 2012. We had 2013 and 2014 and 2015. Three years later, we have a number of members of the Secret Service, violating the Privacy Act, violating DHS and Secret Service procedures. It doesn't seem like we are getting a handle on the cultural problem within the Secret Service.

Mr. ROTH. Senator, Mr. Chairman, thank you for that question.

We have removed people from the Secret Service. You mentioned Cartagena, several were removed in that case. As of today we are in the process of proposing a removal for an individual, unrelated to this. People are removed in the Secret Service.

This Table of Penalties—I know we have referred to it a few times here, but we have used—we have benchmarked that with other agencies, so we are—want to be consistent with what is being done across the board.

Just recently, I published for the first time to our entire workforce our integrity, the discipline over the past year, so they can see what types of cases are out there, are supervisors being disciplined equal to the work force. We are trying to be transparent, again, that communication is critical here, but we are trying to be more transparent, and driving home the point that people will be held accountable.

In this case, they will be held accountable.

Senator JOHNSON. As the Chairman was pointing out, there are an awful lot of protections for the employees, for the actual agents, but again, it is hard to see the accountability.

Do you find that to be a problem? Are you constrained in what actions you would like to take, based on all the protections for the agents? I mean, should we have—should we be looking at the law there, and making sure the agencies have enough power to actually hold people accountable?

Mr. ROTH. Well, I think the excepted service would give us, would allow us to speed up that—the proposals in the discipline process. I know sometimes we are delayed in the process as we move forward.

Senator JOHNSON. So, you would like some ability to take stronger action quicker?

Mr. ROTH. Yes, yes, Mr. Chairman.

Senator JOHNSON. Good. I think we need to take that into account.

Thank you, Mr. Chairman.

Mr. PERRY. The Chair thanks the gentlemen. The Chair now recognizes the gentleman from Mississippi, Mr. Thompson.

Mr. THOMPSON. Thank you very much, Mr. Chairman.

Almost to the Member before me, the conversation has been about the culture of the organization, and I think it speaks to whether or not internally, we can fix it, or do we just cover it up?

I will get to specifics shortly.

Inspector Roth, in your review of the Secret Service, how would you describe the culture within the Service, especially at the Executive level?

Mr. ROTH. As we noted in the report on the access to Chairman Chaffetz's employment record, we found a number of supervisors who, in fact, themselves had access to MCI. To me, that was a very troubling incident; additionally a few people then elevated their concerns, or the fact that this was being used to a high enough level of management for something to be done.

So that was sort of certainly troubling behavior that we identified.

Mr. THOMPSON. So, let me—so, we had senior-level people accessing information, then we had that information being noted by people above those individuals. It is your testimony that nothing happened?

Mr. ROTH. That is correct. I will give two examples, if I may.

The first was the special agent in charge of the Washington field office, came to understand that some of her employees were accessing the MCI to sort-of understand whether or not that rumor existed.

She ordered her individuals—her subordinates to cut it out. I think her exact words were knock it off, or quit fooling around with the MCI database. In fact, that is what occurred in the Washington field office.

Unfortunately, throughout the country, other individuals were doing that, so that would be one example. The second example is the special agent in charge of the Indianapolis field division, who was, frankly, curious why it was that, in his view, Chairman Chaffetz was so hard on Director Clancy.

He, just out of idle curiosity, accessed the database himself to discover, in fact, that Chairman Chaffetz was a prior applicant.

He did nothing with that information, did not elevate it up, or do any other kind of conduct. There are number of examples like that.

Mr. THOMPSON. Thank you very much.

So, Director Clancy, I hope you sense the membership's concern about the culture, and I would hope that going forward, you would take this hearing, as you said, as a moment of instruction to try to fix it.

The men and women deserve it; they do a wonderful job. But it is about leadership, and I think it is absolutely important.

As you know, I have been talking to you since this summer, a little, small issue to some. It is relative to the fact that we found out that there were 643 employees assigned to duty that require a security clearance. They were working for the Department without the completion of the clearances.

I had asked you for the demographics of those individuals. As of this date, I don't have the information.

I know you have been busy, but can you give me some indication when I can expect to receive the demographics of those 643 employees?

Mr. CLANCY. Yes, sir. First of all, my apologies that you have not received that information—640 individuals, I am assuming may be Department-wide, I think within the Secret Service, we did have people working that did not have their security clearances. I think it was much less than that, but we will get you an answer in the coming days on that——

Mr. THOMPSON. Okay. Well, it was Department-wide over a 5-year period, but my point is, some of us run up on men and women around the country who indicate that, I am trying to get employed with the Secret Service, but they tell me, I can't get considered for employment, because I haven't been cleared.

I can't go to training, I can't do a lot of things. But it troubles some of us when we are already employing people whose job requires clearance on the other hand.

So, I don't know if that is favoritism or what. But it is real concerning.

Mr. CLANCY. I will follow up on that, sir.

I can tell you that we don't look at that, diversity, in terms of who gets a security clearance, who does not.

In this case, the one that you referenced—and I will speak for the Secret Service—we were delinquent as we went through this hiring process, we did not get people their security clearances in a timely manner.

Some—and they were assigned to positions outside of Washington, for the most part. But what we have done, now, is we have brought in some contractors, additional 14 contractors, to ensure this never happens again where someone goes through our training and—when they get their graduation—when they graduate, they should have their clearance. So that has been resolved now within the Secret Service.

Mr. THOMPSON. So—it is your testimony that—there is nobody working for the Secret Service right now without a security clearance?

Mr. CLANCY. That is correct. To the best of my knowledge, that is correct.

Mr. THOMPSON. Can you verify that for the committee?

Mr. CLANCY. Yes. Yes, sir.

Mr. THOMPSON. Thank you. I yield back, Mr. Chair.

Mr. PERRY. Chairman thanks the gentleman. The Chairman now recognizes the gentleman from Georgia, Mr. Loudermilk.

Mr. LOUDERMILK. Thank you, Mr. Chairman, and thank you all for being here.

This is especially troubling for me as we look back over the history of this incredible agency, the Service. It is an icon of what I think is American exceptionalism and the actions that we have seen take place—of course, it tarnishes the reputation of the Service, but more so, I think it really tarnishes the image the American people have of what they have always elevated as the exceptional service, not just in the Nation, but in the world. I think it is imperative that we address these issues, not just in hindsight but going forward to make sure that we restore the trust of the American people, the trust of Congress and the trust of the protectees.

Mr. Roth, you said something in your written statement that really struck me here: "The Secret Service has certainly taken steps to address these challenges, but not always successfully. These persistent challenges may not be easy to resolve through expeditious actions, such as suspending employees and issuing new guidance. They may require more fundamental change that addresses the root of the misconduct."

I think that is where we need to focus. What is the root, in your opinion? What is the root of the problem?

Mr. ROTH. When you look at guidance with regard to creating an ethical culture, as they say, it comes in 3 sort-of dimensions. One is tone at the top, which is not just at the very top, but all through leadership of an organization. The leaders have to set the exact right tone. The second is to have a code of conduct and a code of ethics that is truly meaningful. The third is to enforce that code of conduct, you know, in a way that expresses to the rank-and-file that you mean what you say with regard to that tone at the top.

So you have to look at all three of those things. As Director Clancy said, I think the middle part, the code of conduct was not there until Cartagena, and there have been steps that they have taken since Cartagena to establish a more rigorous policy.

So that is certainly an improvement that we think is well-deserved or a positive step in the right direction. But again, it has to be tone all the way through the organization, as well as a meaningful enforcement of that code of conduct.

Mr. LOUDERMILK. I have a time line of misconduct that went back just prior to Cartagena, but it goes back to 2011. Up until that time, I don't recall if—there is misconduct in any organization, but was there a history like we are seeing now, Mr. Roth, that you were aware of, prior to the last, you know, 4 or 5 years?

Mr. ROTH. I am not aware of it. I just don't have any insight into it. Certainly, we are only as good as the audits we do and the investigations we do and we didn't have anything before that.

Mr. LOUDERMILK. Thank you.

Mr. Clancy, I applaud your efforts. You have got a difficult task. You have been in the agency for quite a while. Do you recall that there was the level or the consistency of misconduct previously in the agency or is this just something new?

Mr. CLANCY. I think any agency has always had some misconduct, and the Secret Service has had misconduct in the past. I think it has—more attention has been brought to this misconduct in the last several years and I—and that is a good thing, and I applaud the inspector general's office for that. This has to be brought out in the open, these misconduct episodes, otherwise we won't correct it. So—yes.

Mr. LOUDERMILK. You also—make sure I understood it right. You said that you are trying to—benchmark your disciplinary actions of other agencies. Is that what you were referring to looking at other agencies?

Mr. CLANCY. Yes, my understanding when the Table of Penalties was built out, our legal team worked with other agencies to see what they were doing from a discipline standpoint, what their table penalties were. We took their best ideas, best practices and built ours.

Mr. LOUDERMILK. I would suggest you guys have to be a little stronger, a little better. It is the nature of the work that you do is so important to this Nation. One last thing, I think we have talked a lot about culture in here in the—and that is true.

It is—look, I think what you are getting at is the culture of the agency, it is the esprit de corps. It is—you are in the Secret Service. You have an obligation to uphold the integrity, the honor, and the dignity of this agency. I think that may be what is missing somewhere.

Just real quickly. I was going over this time line and there seems to be a common element with a lot of these. Look at Cartagena. Alcohol was involved. June 2/13—of 2013, alcohol. November 2013, abuse of alcohol. December 2013, alcohol. March, alcohol. June 2014, alcohol. There seems to be this continual cycle of alcohol abuse associated with this, which from my experience in the military, usually indicates that there is a morale issue. I will let you comment and I will yield back after that.

Mr. CLANCY. Yes. You are correct, Congressman. We do have a morale issue, and a lot of it is because of our staffing, and that is one of the things we need to do—work with our staffing so that if we can build up the staffing level, we can get more training, which our people want, get a better quality of life, which will help their morale as well.

But again, to your point here today, the accountability in discipline matters also helps that morale. Are we going to hold people accountable? I will tell you, the episodes since I have been here—you mentioned the March 4 incident where an individual—two individuals after a retirement party drove onto the White House. I can tell you that retirement parties now are—I don't know of any that are taking place. People got that message.

This—what we are talking about today, PII. People are getting this message. So unfortunately, it takes these significant errors—misconduct to resonate sometimes with our people. But I do want to also say one thing. Less than 1 percent of our people are involved in this misconduct. It truly—99 percent, as some of you have mentioned today, are doing the right thing. But that is—and they are working very hard—but we have to focus on that less-than-1-percent, because we are held at a very high—and rightfully so—we are at a high level.

Mr. LOUDERMILK. I hope you can get the Service back to the point to where people aren't doing the right thing because they are afraid of the discipline, but they are doing the right thing because they are dedicated to the job, to the Service, to the spirit of the service and their oath to the Constitution.

Thank you, sir. Mr. Chairman, I yield back.

Mr. PERRY. The Chair thanks the gentleman. The Chair now recognizes the gentlelady from California, Mrs. Torres.

Mrs. TORRES. Thank you, Mr. Chairman. Director Clancy, just to be—to have some statistics here on the record. According to the Partnership for Public Service, the agency is 74 percent male. Is that correct?

Mr. CLANCY. Seventy-five percent. I can—let me just check that real quick. That sounds correct, but I—let me just——

Mrs. TORRES. Seventy-two percent white, leaving it severely out of step with other agencies. Women make up 25 percent of the agency's workforce, but only about 11 percent of the agents and uniformed officers.

Mr. CLANCY. You are correct. Yes.

Mrs. TORRES. You talked about your outreach efforts with universities in targeting certain areas of the Nation. Have you engaged an employment agency to help you or to advise you in finding a more diverse workforce?

Mr. CLANCY. I am not aware that we have done—taken that step yet. It is a—it is an excellent suggestion that we may look into.

I will tell you that when we go to these different areas of the country, we have a very diverse group, recruiting group that goes out to try to encourage females to apply as well as across the board in diversity. So——

Mrs. TORRES. Are you targeting also the military or——

Mr. CLANCY. Yes.

Mrs. TORRES [continuing]. Law enforcement agencies looking for—you know, there are great people working in law enforcement.

Mr. CLANCY. Absolutely. We go to military bases, and again, we run these, what we call ELACs, these Entry-Level Assessment Centers, so that, for example, at a military base, if you want to apply for a job with the Secret Service, we can do a testing initially. If you pass the test, that very day, we can do a super interview of you. If again, it looks like you are a good candidate, then we will move you right to a polygraph, all within a weekend to try to speed up that process.

But absolutely, the military bases—and we have found personally that people that have had a military background serve us very well.

Mrs. TORRES. Well, they have a high work ethic.

Mr. CLANCY. They do.

Mrs. TORRES. They understand the pecking order, they understand the need to serve.

I am disturbed by the incidents. I am happy to hear that it is a reflection on less than 1 percent of the workforce, but by no means does it make me feel better or safer. So would you say you have an agent problem or do you have a management problem?

Mr. CLANCY. It is a management problem, and it starts with me. There is no question it is a management problem, it is a leadership problem that I have got to find an answer to.

Mrs. TORRES. Have you taken steps to ensure that when we are clamping down on agents, that tougher disciplinary actions are taken upon the people who supervise them?

Mr. CLANCY. Yes. Supervisors are held accountable. Again with this—we put this out—again, trying to be transparent—to show our workforce how——

Mrs. TORRES. Are there policies in place to ensure that whistleblowers are protected?

Mr. CLANCY. Yes. Everyone in the service knows that whistleblowers perform a vital function, and they cannot be—there is no retaliation, there is no—you know, you have got to let them go, yes.

Mrs. TORRES. So there are disciplinary steps that the agency takes when the Department rules are violated.

Mr. CLANCY. Yes.

Mrs. TORRES. There are disciplinary steps that the Department takes when our laws are broken.

Mr. CLANCY. Yes.

Mrs. TORRES. The agents are read Miranda rights. Is that what you were referring to in an earlier question?

Mr. CLANCY. No, they are not read Miranda rights. They are read either Kalkines or Garrity, I will let the inspector general correct here if I am wrong on that. But that is what they are read, yes.

Mrs. TORRES. I come from the civilian part of law enforcement, so pardon. So criminal charges are filed, whether they are felony charges or misdemeanor charges. What are your steps? What steps do you take during that process?

Mr. CLANCY. Well, if criminal charges are filed, we typically immediately move to removing the security clearance so that this individual can no longer have access to any of the protected facilities, any access to any of our protectees, of course, or any of our——

Mrs. TORRES. So what happens to the rest of that immediate department that are working with that employee now in the process of a criminal investigation and their supervisors?

Mr. CLANCY. If it is a—at that point, we don't have—we remove all of their badges, we remove their equipment, and then it goes through the normal course of the criminal justice system.

Mrs. TORRES. My time is out. But I—what I am trying to figure out is if you have a rotten apple, how do you ensure that the whole bowl isn't bad?

Mr. CLANCY. Yes. We can remove them very quickly in that case when there are criminal charges. Mr. Chairman, if I could just correct the record for one item. Ranking Member Thompson had asked me about the security clearances. Our agents and officers, some of them that are in training now have not had their clearances settled. They will by graduation.

So anyone who graduates from our academy will have a security clearance. But while they are going through training, some of them may not have.

Mr. THOMPSON. But as of this summer when we talked, that was not the case.

Mr. CLANCY. That is correct. That was not the case. You are absolutely correct. Yes.

Mr. THOMPSON. Thank you.

Mr. PERRY. The Chair thanks the gentlelady. The Chair now recognizes the gentleman from Florida, Mr. Clawson.

Mr. CLAWSON. Sorry to hear about your dad.

Mr. CLANCY. Thank you, sir.

Mr. CLAWSON. Greatest generation.

Mr. CLANCY. It was. I know many here have lost their fathers from that generation, and I think we have all learned from them.

Mr. CLAWSON. Was your dad a vet?

Mr. CLANCY. He was, yes.

Mr. CLAWSON. Yes, I know all about this. I just lost my mom and so, you know, it is the generation that the glass is half-full, put the team first, work hard and go to church on Sunday and the rest answers itself, right?

Mr. CLANCY. Yes, sir. Absolutely.

Mr. CLAWSON. But we were lucky to have those kind of folks.

Mr. CLANCY. Yes, sir. Thank you.

Mr. CLAWSON. Although, you know, we do a little bit for our country now, they—without ever saying it, they remind us that compared to what they did, we don't do much.

Mr. CLANCY. That is correct. Yes, sir.

Mr. CLAWSON. I have full respect and admiration for you and your dad.

I have always thought of organizational culture as being the combination of performance and behavior, and therefore, how your agency and your employees think of themselves is dependent on those two things because they all see it.

When bad behavior is not dealt with quickly, it impacts that culture and how we view each other because it discourages good performers that—you know, that are doing their job every day.

Everything tells me that these incidents of bad behavior ought to be isolated, put up in lights for everyone to see, and that action needs to be taken quickly. That that really is the responsibility of leadership. Therefore when it drags on and on, when it drags on and on, it really sends a bad message to this corporate culture that you referred to earlier.

Why so slow? I mean, you know, systematic, shmistamatic, you know. You are the chief and you have got head of Homeland Security. You know, I mean, let's go. Let's take some actions so that you can do what is right and preserve the culture for you all your great performers. Am I missing something on that? Why so slow?

Mr. CLANCY. No, you are correct. Again, certainly if there is any criminal activity it is much quicker. We can remove their security clearance right away. With other types of misconduct as we are talking about in this case it does take time for the full investigation.

Again, in transparency we had the OIG handle this investigation to do a very thorough investigation, and then once the investigation was completed, then we could move forward with that discipline.

But under Title V, the employees, Federal employees, are given certain rights, and we follow that process, but eventually we get to where we need to be. Eventually we do get to where we need to be.

Mr. CLAWSON. Well, it is going pretty slow for my taste, and I think for the sake of your organization I would be pushing this as hard as I can, because typical folks that run large organizations don't understand this kind of length of time for—you know, it just festers because you don't put it behind you.

Mr. CLANCY. Yes, sir.

Mr. CLAWSON. So, you know, my point is that is let's get going.

I have found in organizational change that if you don't change a third of your people in positions of responsibility you won't change the culture, because they are going to out-wait you. They always out-wait you.

If you change more than 50 percent then you may have a problem with the institutional memory that you discussed earlier.

I am really glad you brought diversity of thought and of experience into your direct reports, but they will out-wait you below that. So just, you know—no rule of thumb is 100 percent for sure, but if I am sitting in your chair and not changing a third of my managers, and you are thinking you are going to change your organization, good luck. Don't believe it.

So you know, I don't know if you have thought of it in numeric terms, but let's get—a performance culture going without washing away the memory of the successes of the past. I am all for having both, and I don't think if you implied this in your early comments, I don't think you—it is one or the other. Change your culture, and preserve the successes of the past. Does that make sense?

Mr. CLANCY. It does, yes, sir.

Mr. CLAWSON. Okay. Is there anything about what I have said that you would disagree with?

Mr. CLANCY. No, I wouldn't sir.

Mr. CLAWSON. Okay. Well, look, we want you to succeed. We could talk all day about whether you should be in the job or not, but you are in the job, and we need you to be successful. So anything I can do, our group, we want you to succeed.

Look, I really like the tone at the top, so let's get them.

Mr. CLANCY. Yes, sir.

Mr. CLAWSON. Thank you.

Mr. PERRY. The Chair thanks the gentleman. The Chair thanks the gentleman. The Chair now recognizes the gentleman from Georgia, Mr. Carter.

Mr. CARTER. Thank you, Mr. Chairman. Thank all of you for being here.

Mr. Clancy, how many times have—when did you get into the office? When did you become the acting director?

Mr. CLANCY. The acting director, October 6, I believe.

Mr. CARTER. October 6?

Mr. CLANCY. Of 2014.

Mr. CARTER. Of 2014. How many times have you appeared before Congress since then?

Mr. CLANCY. I believe this may be my sixth or seventh.

Mr. CARTER. You know, I have been here since January 6 and I think this is the fourth time I have seen you. I am just—I mean, obviously, we have got concerns here. There seems to be an ongoing problem.

Mr. CLANCY. Yes.

Mr. CARTER. As you might know, I am very fortunate to have the Federal Law Enforcement Training Center in Glynco, Georgia, my district. I am familiar with the training that takes place with the Secret Service agents down there, and I think they do an excellent job, but I also want to remind you of the Protective Mission Panel that came out and actually said that the amount of training that the Secret Service agents were getting was far below what is should be.

In fact, I think at one time, they said it was equal to only 25 minutes for each 1,300 uniformed officers?

Mr. CLANCY. Yes.

Mr. CARTER. What are we doing to change that?

Mr. CLANCY. Well, you are absolutely correct, and I have been down to your Federal Law Enforcement Training Center and they do a great job down there, and they help us as we try to build our staffing levels. In terms of what we have done—uniformed division 99% have gone through a building defense exercise training mission—it is a 10-hour block.

Additionally, approximately 700 of our uniformed officers have gone through a 3-day training period where they do their firearms, their emergency medicine, their control tactics—a number of things.

The agents on the President's detail—we have increased the number of agents on the President's detail by November—I am sorry, by the second quarter—early January, we will have increased the numbers there by 85, which is what was recommended by the blue-ribbon panel, and that will help their training.

So we have increased training by 85 percent on the President's detail in this past year.

Mr. CARTER. Okay, well, specifically, let's get to what we are here about today. That is about Chairman Chaffetz and that situation.

Inspector Roth has stated that several of the agents that violated the Secret Service and the Homeland Security policies when they accessed his records. This was criminal offense, don't you think?

Mr. CLANCY. It is on the books as a criminal offense, yes.

Mr. CARTER. It is on the books as a criminal offense.

Tell me what you have done. Have these people been fired? Have they been disciplined at all? A criminal offense by an agency that we hold to the highest standard.

You know, earlier—I am a little bit frustrated by some of the things I have heard, here. Keep in mind that we, up here, are experts at spin. And pivoting. My campaign manager—that was his favorite word—pivot, pivot, pivot.

All of a sudden I heard you talking about data. If the data had been better-protected—give me a break. If they wanted to see this, they were gonna see it, I don't care how the data was protected.

How can you let this go on? Why haven't you fired these people? They knew this was wrong. Don't you agree? Don't you agree? They knew this was wrong.

Mr. CLANCY. I do agree, and certainly, there is misconduct here, the discipline has been proposed for those GS–15 and below. But the data is also important. As a side step.

Mr. CARTER. I understand that, I respect that, and I acknowledge that it is important, that it be protected.

But still, the basic premise here is that they knew what they were doing was wrong.

Mr. CLANCY. Yes. Looking at the OIG report, they should have known what they were doing was wrong. Some of them, I think, will acknowledge——

Mr. CARTER. Should have known? To an agency that we consider to be—to hold at the highest level?

Mr. CLANCY. Right.

Mr. CARTER. I just can't go along with that. I mean, even you yourself said it was inexcusable and unacceptable. It is. It deserves discipline.

Look, I am a small businessman. I have got employees as well, and I can tell you, when something like this happens, and I am not trying to tell you how to run your business, but you know as well as I do that when you got a cancer, you gotta get rid of it. Otherwise, it is going to destroy your whole business. You have got to get rid of this cancer here. You have got to set an example. You have got an opportunity right here to set an example, because what they did was wrong. They knew it was wrong. They deserve discipline. They deserve to be let go.

Mr. CLANCY. They deserve discipline. We do look at the whole picture here, too. The whole person.

Some of these people have spent 28 years with no discipline in their history. Some of them self-reported. Some of them—they are obviously all very remorseful.

But it was wrong? Yes. But we do look at the whole picture and the whole person of their career.

Mr. CARTER. I get that. I want to make sure that the punishment fits the crime and I understand that, and you should look at their whole career. But at the same time, again, you have been here six times since you took office.

Mr. CLANCY. Yes.

Mr. CARTER. We want you to succeed. We don't want to see you fail.

Mr. CLANCY. Yes.

Mr. CARTER. We don't want to see you here anymore. That is essentially it. We want you to do this. We want you to do well, but we gotta have your help.

Mr. Chairman, I yield back.

Mr. PERRY. The Chair thanks the gentleman.

The Chair now recognizes the gentleman from Oklahoma, Senator Lankford.

Senator LANKFORD. Gentlemen, thank you. Long day—we have still got a little ways to go, to be able to bounce you some questions, I appreciate it very much. Let me just state a couple things that I picked up from a lot of the conversation here today. Then I want to walk through multiple questions.

There are a lot of issues with Secret Service. That has been well-documented, and I want to talk about that a little bit.

I would say to you, I do disagree with one of the findings of the panel, I do think someone from the inside needs to be there to be able to fix it.

Someone from the outside that doesn't have the same law-enforcement background or doesn't have the same sense of corporate identity with Secret Service walks in as an outsider and has a different opinion on it. Someone from the inside can walk in and say I am one of us and part of us and can turn some things around.

So I appreciate that you are there because there is obviously work to be done. I am gonna come back to that in just a little bit.

Mr. Roth, let me ask you a question. Is it your sense that for these individuals that accessed this database it was the first time for them to access it—this database like this? Did anyone ever ask them, you know, gosh, did you just happen to say, gosh, maybe I should go look at Jason Chaffetz' records? Someone said, well I think, maybe, we could get access to that.

Or did this look like this was a pattern of behavior, that if they are interested in someone they can go pull it?

Mr. ROTH. I think it ran the gamut depending on the agent we talked to. Some of them didn't think it was wrong at all because what they called it was "our database". It was a Secret Service database unlike, NCIC, or TECS, or one of the other, sort-of larger criminal databases, this was run by the Secret Service and saw nothing wrong with it.

Others didn't understand that it was wrong until after they did it, and then they realized, well, I probably should not have done it.

Senator LANKFORD. There is a training that happens multiple times a year, both orally and electronically—there is, your computer when you start it up there, it says this is for official use only. It is still your perception that some individuals just kind-of ignored all of that and said it is our database, we can do with it what we want.

Mr. ROTH. That is correct.

Senator LANKFORD. Okay. Well, the problem with that is, if they can pull any Member of Congress, if they can pull any individual there, that also means the new neighbor down the street, I can go check my records and see if there is, you know, something on the new neighbor down the street. When their daughter starts dating some new guy they can go pull his family and go pull the records on it.

If this is someone they don't like, they can pull the records.

What we saw from the VA—and we will talk about this with GAO in just a moment—but the VA became a whistleblower there, and we found out that their employees that were then just pulling records, that were medical records on someone they didn't like as a whistleblower in the process.

The challenge that we have here is access to data, you know, it is official and nonofficial and how do we actually direct this.

So, based on your perception and walking through this with Secret Service—is it your perception this has been an on-going issue for some employees just to be able to use that database as just I can go look at it, whether it is official nonofficial, and they blur those lines?

Mr. ROTH. That is the sense we got from at least some of the agents that we interviewed who had accessed the database.

Senator LANKFORD. Okay. Mr. Willemssen, how do we deal with this? Social Security has identified 50 different individuals that were given merit bonuses at the end of the year, but also during the year had accessed information for unofficial purposes and had looked people up.

VA has this issue, which we can talk about in greater length—with someone grabbing information to be able to look at it—that is a whistleblower.

How many agencies have good systems in place to be able to audit, at least, how individuals access these sensitive databases?

Mr. WILLEMSSEN. This particular access problem is probably the most common issue that we see when we are doing detailed information security audits. Too many people have access to things they don't need access to. It is not part of their job description. They don't have a need to know, but yet, they are given access.

So access is a real issue. It is one that we—I would say that is probably the most frequent one we come up with.

Another issue that is interesting in this case is when you are collecting PII you—one of the things you do is end up scheduling a records notice with NARA—National Archives and Records Administration—to among other things, tell them how long you are going to keep the files before you dispose of it.

I was kind-of curious about why an application file from 2003 would be kept 12 years later. Those kinds of things should be disposed of fairly quickly. Hopefully, that is part of what the Service will be doing going forward.

You are supposed to schedule those records out and dispose of them at a certain date. Sometimes 1 year, sometimes 5 years.

Senator LANKFORD. Can you pause on that?

Mr. Clancy, has that been taken care of at this point? There are two different sets of information. Both the electronic records that are not applicable anymore, and paper records, because it is my understanding that are still some offices though the access point has been changed electronically, if you go into a file room, those old application files may still be there in paper form, as well.

Has that been dealt with as well?

Mr. CLANCY. Yes, we are moving forward too, for example, the applicants. Every 2 years those files will be purged. Right now there is an investigation going on with the inspector general, so some of that will be delayed slightly until they're through the investigation, but that is the plan forward. Also, again, with the applicants in mind, 95 percent of the people that had access before no longer will have access because of the new system.

Senator LANKFORD. Is that both paper and electronic for those offices around the country, do they still have access to paper records—somewhere in a filing cabinet?

Mr. CLANCY. I will have to get back to you with a good solid answer on that. I think we have moved away from a lot of the paper, but let me give you a better answer.

Senator LANKFORD. Okay. That would be something wise to be able to evaluate as well. Both the electronic version, the access points, and then obviously the paper version to make sure that that is also purged. It may be, just if you have access to that room, you also have access to those files, and it is part of the challenge here.

Let me come back to Mr. Willemssen.

Which agency would you identify and say this agency is a good model example of how to handle personal identifiable information? They are auditing well, they are tracking well, they are a model agency?

Mr. WILLEMSSEN. Don't have one. No model agency.

Senator LANKFORD. That is somewhat depressing.

Mr. WILLEMSSEN. Yes, it is. Now, the more optimistic note, since the OPM cyber disaster, this has become a major priority. OMB has charged up, it has definitely elevated its priority on this. Agency heads now recognize that this is a critical issue that needs to be addressed.

You know, and when we first announced the information security area as high-risk, first few years I was told, you know, you are Chicken Little, the sky is falling.

I don't hear that anymore.

Senator LANKFORD. Sky fell.

Mr. WILLEMSSEN. Yes.

Senator LANKFORD. Okay. So the challenge that we have here is dealing with—let me just give you one example of VA. This is something GAO has for years and years identified issues with VA.

Mr. WILLEMSSEN. Yes, sir.

Senator LANKFORD. How does this get better? How do we prevent unauthorized access of medical information and of private information for our veterans?

Mr. WILLEMSSEN. Veterans Affairs has a significantly high percentage of systems that are considered high-impact systems—that is, the disclosure of data or modification of the data because of the medical records, is considered to be very severe in terms of its possible impact if it is lost, stolen, or reviewed by others.

Given that, you have to put much stricter controls in place, including monitoring users and what they are doing, and if they have any atypical patterns in use, and the——

Senator LANKFORD. Is this just an audit, or is this an algorithm that is created?

Mr. WILLEMSSEN. This is an audit and an algorithm. You can do it automatically.

Senator LANKFORD. Right.

Mr. WILLEMSSEN. It is contained in the National Institute for Standards and Technology guidance for high-impact systems. Like I said, VA has a significant percentage of high-impact systems where you have got to put these kind of controls in place to try to prevent the kind of situations that you described.

Senator LANKFORD. Mr. Chairman, I would like—I don't know if we are going to do a second round of questions, but I do have additional questions for Director Clancy as well.

Mr. PERRY. If you don't mind, I will suspend.

Thank you, sir, and I will suspend your questions at the time and recognize Mrs. Watson Coleman for a second round.

Mrs. WATSON COLEMAN. Mr. Chairman, you know, I know we were here. I know that my colleagues wanted us to sort-of focus on what happened to Chairman Chaffetz.

I think if I were him—if I were he, I would probably want this to just go away now. Take care of the business that needs to be taken care of, discipline the people that need to be disciplined, learn the lessons that you need to learn, but, you know, I just really don't think he needs to have this or wants to have this as a continuing story.

But it does speak to other issues that we are identifying, and it does speak to a culture or way of thinking or way of doing business or the way we—they—we perceive ourselves on the inside that needs to be addressed. I know you have expectations for that changing.

I would like to know any steps that you are actually taking to change the culture in the form of action. What happens with your executive level? What happens with the level beneath that, the supervisory level? What happens with the rank-and-file level?

How are you addressing the need to get our agency to think more differently about how we come to work? What we do at work? We don't sleep at work. We don't sex text under any circumstances. You know, we don't look into files that we don't have a responsibility, a need to look into.

Is there going to be some sort of a fail-safe mechanism that shows when the file is being accessed by someone who shouldn't be, or has no reason to be? I would like to know some steps that you are taking.

Thank you. Thank you, Mr. Chairman.

Mr. CLANCY. I just think, in terms of the overall culture here, one of the things we are doing is we are trying to have our workforce take ownership of this agency. It is their agency, and—let me just give you one example.

Just 3 or 4 weeks ago, we started a new program. It is a crowdsourcing type of service on our intranet where our agents and our officers and all of our employees—professional staff can send in ideas, suggestions, what we should be doing better, what should we be looking at, and then they get other people from the workforce looking at that, and they can "like" that, for—better term, and then it forces the executive staff to look at that.

We have seen this as a very positive—already within a few weeks, we have had close to 200 hits of—we call it Spark—where people have taken ownership of their agency.

Now, I think that is where we have got to get to that point. It is management, it is my leadership, but additionally, it is the individuals who have to take ownership of this agency. I will say again, 99 percent of our people do have that ownership.

Mrs. WATSON COLEMAN. So, Mr. Clancy, I have been in the Executive branch of Government, and I know it takes that kind of expectation, but it takes a plan of action, and it takes whether or not you are hiring people from the outside who look at these issues and work through groups, and you work down through the organization.

So at some point I would like to know if you are planning to do those kinds of action steps.

Then the last question is—I really do want to know—is there some sort of way that there is a notification of accessing information when you are not—when it is out of order for what you are doing, it is not related to your case? Your identification number to get into it signals whether or not you are or are not the right person to be accessing this information? As a follow-up to Senator Lankford's concerns.

Mr. CLANCY. My understanding is—and the other gentlemen in here may be able to answer this better—but it requires constant monitoring and auditing, and there is no automatic notice that someone has accessed someone's data inappropriately. It has to be constant monitoring.

Each——

Mrs. WATSON COLEMAN. Who——

Mr. CLANCY [continuing]. There is an administrator for each of these buckets of information, and that administrator has to control who has access—who has the need to know that information.

So it is up to the administrator—so with our human resources, we have approximately 260 that would have access to our applicant data with this new system, and that administrator would have to ensure that anyone else who enters has access they have approved.

Mrs. WATSON COLEMAN. Thank you. Did you want to say something to this, Mr. Roth—respond to this?

Mr. ROTH. If I may—yes, if I may, just as an example, the DHS TECS system is one in which, for example, if Director Clancy had created a record there and then I accessed that record, Director Clancy would get an e-mail that I was the one who accessed the record.

So not only what Director Clancy was talking about, which is—you know, you can run reports by the system administrator, but there are also sort of real-time controls on modern IT systems that weren't present in the MCI system.

Mrs. WATSON COLEMAN. Thank you, Mr. Chairman. I yield back.

Mr. PERRY. Chair thanks the gentlelady from New Jersey. Chair recognizes the gentleman Mr. Lankford.

Senator LANKFORD. Thank you.

I think the audit system is gonna be the key. At whatever percentage that that is, to be able to have, for this computer at this spot, here is everything that you ran, and that they know at some point, someone is going to just spot-audit.

You can't go through all of it. There is not a need to go through all of it. But just the simple accountability that sits out there somewhere, to know there is an algorithm that is running, to say, "hey, there is a search for files that don't seem to be consistent with official records."

There is a spot audit occasionally, that you may come in and face discipline, saying, "you pulled records from your neighbor down the street, or from someone you don't like." All those things, I think, just become important.

We have a tremendous number of people that work in the Federal workforce that are great people, that generally love the country and love to be able to do what their job is. The problem is these small—as Mr. Clancy, as you mentioned—the 1 percent on it.

I had to smile as we were walking through some of the conversation about Secret Service and picking on Secret Service today. I hope we are really not picking on you. This has become the latest example of multiple examples, whether that be VA or Social Security or others became the visual example again.

But I have to tell you, as I have listened to some of the conversation on the dais about challenges with public-relations nightmares and employees not doing their job and alcohol abuse and everything else, we could, quite frankly, flip the tables, and y'all could hold a hearing on Members of Congress and have the same accusation.

I would assure you it is more than 1 percent of the Members of Congress have some of these exact same issues. So this issue is not—is a human behavior issue, but it is also a professionalism issue of taking the task seriously.

So, Mr. Clancy, I am going to give you an unfair list, and just to be able to walk through a few things, and I am going to tell you this in advance—as I have tried to start walking through some of the issues and the recommendations for the Secret Service—it is the oldest law—oldest general law enforcement entity in our country. It is an incredibly valuable resource to our Nation.

But my fear is some changes that have been put in place over the past several decades—it is not on your watch—have brought about some morale shifts on it. What I am trying to figure out is how do we shift morale back, and how do we get on top of this? Otherwise, it is Whack-a-Mole with the different issues all the time.

Overtime rules seem to come up over and over again as I talk to different agents and individuals. Getting some sort of standard practice with your counterpart agencies. Accountability of leadership, so if there is a bad actor, everyone knows that is not tolerable in our agency.

When you actually confront issues, everyone knows that is the standard and we are going to live up to it. If there is a bad apple, as has been stated, in the group, or someone that is flippant about it, everyone kind of works down to that level.

Priority of new equipment and technology. I find that Secret Service is not getting the top priority for some of the newest technology and newest equipment among our DHS law enforcement, and I think it is demeaning. That sends a false message to Secret Service that they are not as valuable as some of the other aspects of DHS.

Their responsibilities seem to be getting cluttered instead of a clarity, where it has been historically, for protection and for counterfeit duties. There seems to be other duties that seem to be kind of creeping into it that distract from the core mission here.

The consistent career track—that seems to be a consistent theme that I have heard over and over again, that the career track seems to change, so no one really knows what path they are on here. Am I off on any of these at this point?

Mr. CLANCY. No, you are correct, and I will just comment on your last—the career track. We did bring in a workforce of agents at different levels to try to look at the best career track moving forward, and we have just announced, a couple months ago, the new career track for our agents so that they can plan their future.

That has been one of the problems. You don't know if you are going to come to Washington, or will you be able to go to Texas. So we are, again, listening to our workforce, trying to find solutions.

Senator LANKFORD. That is one of the things you can do if you are on the inside and you know full well what is happening. But I would encourage in the career track—and y'all have already examined this, and go from there—the possibility that individuals that are on a previous career track still could finish that out.

Mr. CLANCY. Yes.

Senator LANKFORD. They can be grandfathered into that, or, if they choose to shift to the other one, they could choose that as well. That gives them the option and not feel like the new guys got the new stuff, or whatever it may be, but also have something to say, "I started on this, I can actually complete this and not feel like the rules are changing on me again" as they walk through.

This corporate identity is extremely important, and is extremely valuable. What I fear is that there is a growing sense of lack of importance of people that are incredibly important to our Nation.

I never want Secret Service folks to feel like they just guard doors for a living. They don't. They have an incredibly valuable role, and the morale, and the—what you set—and the role and the standard that you set will be incredibly important for years to come.

If there is a silver lining in this, historically, Secret Service have had a really bad time when a President was shot. No one has been shot.

There are just some things that were messed up, and this is unique moment for—publicly for the Secret Service to reevaluate again, and go, "Who are we? Where are we going? What is our clear task?"

I would encourage you, if there are issues in working with DHS and in the scheme of things, these committees need to know it, because we want to make sure that all of the DHS families all feel equal levels of importance.

Your Secret Service transitioned pretty quickly, I guess, from working in the Treasury to DHS and all the restructuring and you are now one of many rather than the big dog of Treasury. That has both benefits and challenges, and we need to know and to have some way to be able to help communicate in that so that we can help actually engage in this because we are not only advocates, but we are accountability in the process.

Today probably feels more like accountability, but we also have the desire to be advocates on these roles. So we will need to know that. Is that fair?

Mr. CLANCY. That is fair, Mr. Chairman. If I could comment on one thing there, sir.

Senator LANKFORD. Yes, sir.

Mr. CLANCY. Just to give you some comfort—I know it has given me comfort, but I went through this papal visit as well as the U.N. General Asembly. I traveled with the Pope and I can tell you, as I talk to our agents, our officers and our professional staff, this was a defining moment for our agency. As I talk to these people, I looked in their eyes, they wanted to be successful. They know the issues that have been highlighted, and rightfully so, over the past several years.

This was an unprecedented time in our history and our people were determined to make this successful and we did this for NSSEs without incident, and our people felt very proud about that and I am very proud of our workforce.

Now having said that, we have got to correct these other things too, and we will, but we have got people that are working very hard for the American people.

Senator LANKFORD. Yes, you do, and we acknowledge that and we understand that. But we also don't want anything to distract it.

Mr. CLANCY. Yes, sir.

Senator LANKFORD. Mr. Willemssen, let me ask you this as well. When we are talking about databases and we are talking about access points, is there any independent agency or agency that is an Executive agency that you think has a higher risk or has no system of tracking this, old or new, that you look at and say these—of the high-risk, these are the highest-risk?

Part of my question—are the independent agencies—do we know for certain that they have auditing process? Because they handle incredibly sensitive financial data on Americans.

Mr. WILLEMSSEN. I would point to those agencies who have the most PII, personally identifiable information, as reason to make sure that they are doing everything they can to protect that.

So you start with Social Security Administration, who has PII on almost every citizen. Veterans Affairs you have already mentioned, definitely an issue. Department of Education, probably somewhat overlooked because they have a tremendous amount of PII because of the student loans, not only on the student, but sometimes on the parents.

So I would be most concerned about where the PII is the most significant.

Senator LANKFORD. Let me ask you about things like SEC or CFPB, fairly new entity for CFPB, they have a tremendous amount of data.

Mr. WILLEMSSEN. Yes.

Senator LANKFORD. Do we know, on their employees, how they have access and the limitations that they have?

Mr. WILLEMSSEN. We know that they have at least three sets of data collection that includes PII, maybe more. Arbitration case records, bank-deposit account and transaction-level data and store-front payday loans.

Senator LANKFORD. What is their auditing process for their employees inappropriately accessing that?

Mr. WILLEMSSEN. That is something we will have—we can follow up on. We did make a recommendation in terms of the—we previously had done work and we made a recommendation related to their privacy-impact assessment.

Whenever you collect PII, you have got to do a privacy-impact assessment that lets everyone know what are we collecting, why are we collecting it, how are we going to use it, how are we not going to use it, and when are we going to dispose of it.

They had not fully done those when we had done our work, so made a recommendation on that, and that is something I can follow up on and see where they are at.

Senator LANKFORD. I know CFPB has just requested, again, another incredibly large jump in the amount of information that they are gathering on Americans and gathering on databases. That seems to exceed even what was originally designed in Dodd-Frank.

Mr. WILLEMSSEN. Well, it may be more than what we had mentioned in our report, then. They may have further expanded it.

Senator LANKFORD. It is a fairly recent expansion request for additional information. What we are trying to figure out is who has access to that, how often do they have access to that?

Mr. WILLEMSSEN. We can follow up for you on the that.

Senator LANKFORD. That would be very helpful to this Congress.

Mr. WILLEMSSEN. Yes, sir.

Senator LANKFORD. Gentlemen, I thank you for your participation today.

Mr. PERRY. The Chair thanks the gentleman from Oklahoma.

Before I close out, I have got a couple questions. Mr. Willemssen, you know, you are from the Government Accountability Office and I read through your information. I am just wondering if you can provide any clarity on other agencies regarding penalties, regarding accountability for actions that have been—that they have engaged in regarding security clearances? That might be out of your wheelhouse, and if it is, that is——

Mr. WILLEMSSEN. Well, I can talk about numerous—some of the major incidents over time. Probably the first major incident we had with inappropriate browsing was at the IRS in the mid-1990s. Several employees decided to start browsing celebrities' tax returns, and actually, as a result of that, there was an act passed, the Taxpayer Browsing Protection Act, 1997. That, among other things, has penalties of up to a $1,000 fine and imprisonment of not more than 1 year.

Mr. PERRY. Do you know if anybody was ever prosecuted under that? And was subjected to those penalties at all?

Mr. WILLEMSSEN. Do not know that, sir, but I can—we can follow up on that with the IRS.

Mr. PERRY. Well, I—actually, I wish you would, just so we know.

Director, you also mentioned that—I think you are—there are some limitations, right, to what you can do regarding accountability, regarding punishment for actions that are beneath the standard? Is that correct?

Mr. CLANCY. Yes. We are not able to fire at will.

Mr. PERRY. You are not—okay. So we need to know, the members of this board and Congress in general needs to know what you need us to do for you to be successful, for you to manage your force, okay? We need your direct recommendations and that is, as I have said so many times in the room, we want you to be successful, and if we are standing in the way, you need to let us know what we can do, what we should do, so that you could be successful.

You know, I have served for over 30 years the United States military, if you are familiar with the Army, and I guarantee you if there is a question of your security clearance and your activity regarding the security clearance, that is suspended on an interim basis, pending an investigation. If you are found to have been at fault, and have breached, that is very serious. It incredibly serious for the most minor infractions. It is not meant to be a culture of punishment and fear, but it is meant to keep honest people honest and to raise to the level of importance those things that should be important.

I would just suggest that maybe that would be something that you might want to look at for suspension of security clearances, which I would imagine in your business, a suspension of a security clearance, certainly on an interim basis—maybe on an interim basis, but absolutely on a permanent basis means loss of employment because you can't be employed without it, right? And——

Mr. CLANCY. That is correct, yes, sir.

Mr. PERRY. That is correct, right? So that gets to where we want to be. I would also say this. In looking at some of the testimony, we are concerned about how fast you are getting the information. You are the top dog and you are in charge and I get it. But I will tell you this too. Whether it is in my family, whether or, whether it is in the military, whether I was running my business, bad information, bad news does not get better with time.

There must be a culture of something happened, and who needs to know and we get the information up to the top of the chain as quickly as possible because you have got to be able to do your job. You can't do it without the information. If your subordinates don't know that that is your expectation, then we are going to have—we are going to have this continuation of this, which none of us want.

You are sitting here in front of us and you are defending your agency and your agents, as we expect you to, as you should. You will probably also note that 95 percent of your time will be spent on 5 percent of your people. Director, I have been out to your operation and I have been well impressed and all of us really want to hold up the Secret Service as the standard. We want that. Americans really desperately want that.

So these things are incredibly hurtful, so when we hear them in the news, they are hurtful. There is a bigger picture here and I think your agents, your employees need to understand it is not their system. It is the taxpayers' database, and is not their information, it is those individuals' information.

You don't own it, those individuals own it. To use it willy-nilly is reprehensible in an age when, as the Senator talked about, your—all these information that the governments gather, the information that the private sector is gathering and what happens to it and who owns it and the force of law under the ACA, which says you must submit your information.

To think and to wonder that somebody might be using that for their personal whatever, that is a problem. That is a problem for the American citizen trusting their Government, and your employees have a direct connection to that. They must—in my opinion, they must understand that.

I want to just speak to this—you have been questioned a couple times on diversity and also on filling your ranks and in keeping your people employed and keeping them incentivized and so on and so forth. We understand that you have challenges, just like everybody does, complying with the law and filling your ranks with the people that you want to have there. We understand that. I would say from this person's perspective, we want you, I want you to get the best. You get the best, all right? You get the best to do the job.

Finally, I noticed a couple times you said you are trying to be consistent with other agencies. I will tell you this, sir. I understand where you want to be, but this is the Secret Service, the premier organization of your type in the United States Government, in the world.

How about if you lead? If you can't find somebody that meets the standards you want to set in your agency around the Government agencies, go outside. Make your own standard. If you need help from us, you need to ask for it, all right?

Thank you very much for your time here. Gentlemen—again—I thank you, the witnesses all for your very valuable testimony and for the Members and their questions. Members may have some additional questions for the witnesses and we will ask that you respond to those in writing.

Without objection, this subcommittees stand adjourned.

[Whereupon, at 12:02 p.m., the subcommittees were adjourned.]

APPENDIX

Question 1a. According to Secret Service officials, USSS policies related to accessing and disclosing PII are available in the Secret Service ethics manual distributed to USSS personnel and on the Secret Service intranet site. In addition, Secret Service employees are required to recertify their ethics training yearly.

What percentage of the workforce actually completes the yearly recertification and what audit measures are in place to ensure the workforce is recertifying?

Answer. Employees certify annually that they are aware of a variety of agency policies via the SSF 3218, to include the agency manual sections on Employee Responsibilities and Conduct, Table of Penalties, and Discipline. These forms are subject to audit when agency offices are inspected by the Office of Professional Responsibility's Inspection Division.

With respect to ethics training, in calendar year 2014, the Office of Chief Counsel (LEG) provided ethics training to 100% of those employees required to receive it. In calendar year 2015, LEG targeted a goal of 100% compliance and has provided in-person training to a total of 587 employees. LEG reports the results of its training efforts annually to the Office of Government Ethics.

With respect to required on-line training, the table below reflects the percentage of the workforce that has completed each of the 3 identified courses that involve employee conduct and/or treatment of personal information.

PRIVACY & PII TRAINING COMPLETIONS FOR USSS IN FISCAL YEAR 2015

Course Title	Privacy at DHS: Protecting Personal Information	Decision Making Elements	IT Security Awareness
	This on-line course is required annually	March 2015 was official rollout for this yearly required on-line course	This on-line course is required annually
Employee Completions *	5,604	5,563	5,385
Percent of the Workforce Completions for Fiscal Year 2015 (Numbers include active and inactive employees with no duplicates)	89%	88%	86%

* Totals represent "unique employee completion" (both active/inactive employees with no duplicates).

The enforcement mechanisms (or audit measures) to ensure the on-line courses are completed are multi-tiered:

(1) *Self-Check.*—Employee logs onto learning management system (LMS) regularly to ensure he/she is taking the courses by due date(s).

(2) *Supervisory Check.*—Supervisor logs onto LMS and reviews his/her employee progress and/or the office Training Coordinator provides the supervisor(s) with a non-compliant list.

(3) *2nd Supervisory Check (during evaluation process).*—Supervisor conducts the employee's mid-year and final evaluation, reviews the status of prescribed/required training, and discusses any other training the employee may need or want to improve or develop his/her skill-set.

(4) *Inspection Division Audit.*—All field offices and protective divisions are inspected every 4 years by the Inspection Division (ISP). During the ISP review, on-line training is audited to determine whether all employees have completed mandatory LMS training.

Question 1b. What follow-up is conducted for non-compliant employees who fail to complete the training?

Answer. Employees found to be non-compliant with required courses could be held accountable in performance evaluations and could be subject to discipline in accordance with the established Table of Penalties.

Question 1c. How do senior officials hold mid-level management accountable for ensuring their subordinates are aware of and operating within USSS ethics policies?

Answer. Senior officials are responsible for communicating their expectations, including adherence to Secret Service ethics policies, to mid-level management during regular interactions, mid-year reviews, and final reviews. Failure on the part of mid-level management to ensure their subordinates are aware of and operating within those ethics policies could be reflected in the manager's performance review and could result in discipline under the Table of Penalties.

Question 2a. According to USSS staff, in 2007, an NSA review called for the MCI system to be upgraded. Despite this recommendation, the Secret Service did not begin to take any action related to upgrading the system until 2011 and the MCI upgrade was not completed until June of this year. Since fiscal year 2011, when the upgrade began, Congress has appropriated over $227 million for USSS IT transformation.

How much of this appropriated sum was used to modernize the MCI system?

Answer. The MCI migration was part of the Mainframe Applications Refactoring project which utilized approximately $13.49 million to complete the migration into modernized systems with security controls and audit logging. The out-year sustainment costs are $2 million per year.

Question 2b. Why did it take so long for MCI to be upgraded and why did USSS wait 4 years after the NSA review to begin the upgrade? Was it a funding issue, a personnel issue, an acquisition issue, a technical issue, or something else?

Answer. The MCI upgrade was dependent on the availability of modernization funds to obtain the appropriate assets to complete the project. These funds were needed to obtain the equipment and skilled personnel to take on the effort of transitioning from a period of technological stabilization to modernization. The Secret Service's Information Integration and Technology Transformation ("IITT") program was established in fiscal year 2010. In recognition of the limitations of MCI and other mainframe applications, the Secret Service initiated the Mainframe Application Refactoring ("MAR") project in 2011 to assess the existing 48 applications residing on the mainframe and migrate necessary capabilities and accompanying data to a non-mainframe, secure, highly-available and compartmentalized environment. DHS estimated the project would take 10 years to complete. The Secret Service accelerated the MAR project in 2013 and was able to achieve project closure on June 24, 2015.

Question 3a. Since becoming Director, you have launched a series of communication initiatives to open lines of communication between senior management and the rank-and-file USSS employees. These initiatives include focus groups, an Ombudsman question line, and the new Spark! tool. These actions would appear to "clearly communicate agency priorities" and "create more opportunities for offices and agents to provide input on their mission" as recommended by the Protective Mission Panel.

What kind of buy-in and participation in these initiatives have you seen from the rank-and-file employees?

Question 3b. What reforms, either completed or in process, have been brought about as a result of these initiatives?

Answer. Given that sub-questions a and b are closely related, the Secret Service will address these together.

Spark!

On October 19, 2015, the Secret Service introduced the Spark! Program, which is a crowdsourcing, web-based communication platform that provides every employee with a virtual voice to make suggestions, share ideas, and find solutions to elevate our mission and continue to improve the agency. This new program allows senior management to communicate directly with the entire workforce on what initiatives are being pursued and what the agency's priorities are as they relate to the posts on the site. The Spark! Program, although still in its infancy, has already seen participation by 3,374 employees, which is 54% of the workforce.

Focus Groups

In October 2014, the Secret Service selected Eagle Hill Consulting as the primary contractor to conduct a Work/Life Integration Assessment beginning in November 2014. Eagle Hill conducted focus group interviews throughout the Nation with Secret Service employees. A survey was distributed garnering participation from approximately 57% of the total Secret Service population. Eagle Hill completed its assessment in December 2015.

Throughout this engagement, frequent communication with the Secret Service workforce has been essential in providing the workforce transparent, accurate information about the status of the work/life assessment and its results. Regular updates from the director via e-mail and a permanent work/life integration webpage on the Secret Service intranet inform employees about near-term measures and next steps as the organization responds to critical quality-of-life concerns. For example, an agency-wide communication from the director in response to focus group findings conveyed new initiatives to provide greater clarity and transparency regarding the special agent reassignment process, career track and promotion guidelines for law enforcement personnel, permanent change of station move process, hardship policy, and enhancements to the organization's telework policy.

Now that the Eagle Hill engagement has concluded, focus group results, survey data, and external research into Federal agency work/life best practices will be presented to the Secret Service Executive Staff. These efforts will inform a series of final recommendations to be developed by Eagle Hill regarding development of a permanent Work/Life Integration Program. Through the recently-established Work/Life Working Group chaired by the deputy director, the organization will consider in detail each of the recommendations and in 2016 begin developing appropriate programmatic responses to enhance workforce quality of life on a long-term basis.

Question 4a. The Protective Mission Panel recommended replacing the fence surrounding the White House, stating, "a better fence can provide time, and time is crucial to the protective mission. Every additional second of response time provided by a fence that is more difficult to climb makes a material difference in ensuring the President's safety and protecting the symbol that is the White House." The Panel also suggested the fence be replaced as quickly as possible. Thus far however, the only changes have been the addition of some spikes and bike racks which push the fence line out a few feet.

Please provide an update on the USSS plans to replace the fence.

Answer. In response to the September 19, 2014 incident and the findings of the Protective Mission Panel, the Secret Service pursued interim and long-term actions needed to address White House fence vulnerabilities.

To immediately increase the difficulty associated with jumping the fence, the Secret Service installed temporary security enhancements on the existing fence. These temporary measures were meant to bolster security needs while a long-term solution is designed and implemented.

To permanently address all identified fence vulnerabilities, the Secret Service, through the National Park Service (NPS), initiated an engineering study to examine physical changes that would increase the structural integrity of the White House fence against both individuals and an organized, dynamic attack. The study concluded on May 28, 2015. Based on the results of the study, the Secret Service decided to pursue the design of two different permanent fence options. Both options will be developed concurrently and in enough detail so that they can be presented to NPS, the National Capital Planning Commission (NCPC), the Commission of Fine Arts (CFA), the District of Columbia State Historic Preservation Officer (DC SHPO), and others for consideration. Award of the contract for the permanent fence design took place in September 2015.

Question 4b. When do you expect the project to be completed and at what cost?

Answer. Prior to completion of the study and the latest fence-jumping incident on November 26, 2015, the Secret Service estimated that design, acquisition/contracting, and construction of the permanent fence project would take a minimum of 28 months, potentially longer if the NPS, the NCPC, and the CFA require revisions/modifications to the proposed design.

After completion of the study, negotiations with the architect/engineer responsible for the design of the permanent fence, additional discussions with NPS (the Government agency with responsibility/jurisdiction over the fence), as well as a review of the November 26, 2015 fence-jumping incident, the Secret Service now believes this project will take longer than 28 months.

The concepts for the permanent fence design were based in part on the security/anti-climb features incorporated into the interim fence upgrades that were present during the November 26, 2015 fence-jumping incident. Based on the results of this incident, the Secret Service plans to re-evaluate the permanent design concepts, as well as assess the effectiveness of additional features to be incorporated into the new permanent fence.

The fiscal year 2016 Consolidated Appropriations Act included $8.2 million (available for 2 years) for security enhancements to the White House fence. This estimate was developed prior to the completion of the study and design phase of the project. Once the permanent design is developed and additional details about the permanent fence are known, the Secret Service will be better positioned to provide an estimated total cost to replace the existing White House fence.

Question 5. As stated in the OIG addendum issued in October, Deputy Director Magaw said he informed you on March 25 of the rumor that Rep. Chaffetz had applied to the Secret Service. Why did you not take immediate steps to learn more information about the nature and validity of the rumor? Why did Deputy Director Magaw not inform you that the rumor was the result of improper access and distribution of PII information in the MCI database?

Answer. As previously reported to the DHS OIG, on March 25, 2015, Deputy Director Magaw notified me of the rumor surrounding Representative Chaffetz's application with the Secret Service. At that time, I had no reason to believe that any Secret Service databases, including MCI, had been accessed to obtain this information. Like Deputy Director Magaw, I believed it to be an unsubstantiated rumor and nothing more. In fact, both Deputy Director Magaw and I were not aware that a Secret Service database had been accessed until April 2, 2015. That same day, I sent an official message to the entire workforce directing them to immediately cease all unauthorized access and dissemination of sensitive information.

On April 3, 2015, I convened a meeting with his executive staff to inform them of the situation. At this meeting, I reiterated the importance of protecting sensitive PII and informed them that any violations to Secret Service policy would not be tolerated.

Subsequently, the DHS OIG's investigation revealed that subsequent to the April 2, 2015 official message, no additional personnel accessed Representative Chaffetz's information.

Question 6. Why did Secret Service maintain applicant information from 12 years prior in its systems? Why was such information not purged or sent for archiving?

Answer. At the time of the events in question, the Secret Service was still governed by records retention schedules requiring this type of information be retained for 20 years. Due to the fact that these schedules were vetted, approved, and signed by the National Archives and Records Administration (NARA), adherence to these schedules was a matter of legal compliance. New NARA-approved retention schedules have now replaced the legacy schedules, and information relating to applicants who are not hired is held only for 2 years, unless a formal background investigation is conducted. If a formal background investigation is conducted, the case file is held for 5 years.

QUESTIONS FROM RANKING MEMBER BENNIE G. THOMPSON FOR JOSEPH P. CLANCY

Question 1. Director Clancy, it was recently reported that a Uniformed Division officer was arrested for sending pornographic images to a minor. Prior to his arrest, the Secret Service Office of Professional Responsibility became aware of the investigation and suspended the officer's security clearance and took his service weapon. How did the Secret Service work with the authorities to make sure that the investigation of this officer was not compromised since the Secret Service took action before the officer was arrested and indicted?

Answer. On November 6, 2015, the Maryland State Police (MSP) contacted the Secret Service to advise that they, in conjunction with the Delaware State Police (DSP), and ICE's Homeland Security Investigations (HSI) were conducting an investigation into potential criminal misconduct by a USSS employee.

That day, representatives from the Office of Professional Responsibility contacted the DHS OIG and advised that the USSS employee was assigned to the White House Complex and the allegations against the employee posed significant National security concerns. DHS OIG requested that the USSS not take any administrative action against the USSS employee as law enforcement involved in this investigation was planning to execute a search warrant in less than 2 weeks. However, due to the criminal nature of the allegations and the sensitivity of the position held by the employee, the USSS made the decision to immediately suspend the employee's security clearance and place him on administrative leave.

Question 2. Director Clancy, it was recently reported that 2 USSS agents were observed during a routine systems check sleeping at their duty stations. This observation was so concerning, the DHS inspector general issued a management alert, citing long overtime shifts, travel fatigue, and a lack of water as some of the causes.

What plans do you have in place to address overtime concerns, particularly in the Uniformed Division?

Answer. The Uniformed Division continues to evaluate overtime usage across all Uniformed Division Branches with the goal of equitably minimizing extensive overtime shifts and preserving days off. Each Uniformed Division Branch manually tracks the overtime accumulation of each officer per pay period as a current management practice. Every effort is made to staff critical vacant assignments with personnel who volunteer to work overtime prior rather than forcing personnel to work overtime.

The concept of consolidating all Uniformed Division scheduling offices to gain efficiencies and cross level overtime between Branches is currently under review. In addition, specialty function Uniformed Division personnel are being temporarily reassigned to fill critical assignments in an effort to reduce the amount of overtime hours as well as cancelled days off.

Variable assignments, such as temporary magnetometer screening details, typically result in short-notice protective travel and incur overtime for personnel to replace or "backfill" Uniformed Division personnel on TDY status. The Uniformed Division, as well as the Office of Protective Operations, are reviewing current planning practices in order to determine temporary magnetometer detail requirements as early as possible in the protective advance planning process in order to minimize overtime as a result of short-notice TDY travel.

Question 3. The Protective Mission Panel suggested an increase of 200 Uniformed Division officers as well as 85 Protective Division officers. Has the Secret Service increased staffing since this recommendation and by how many? Will this increase in staffing help decrease the number of officers needed for long overtime shifts, particularly in the Uniformed Division?

Answer. As of December 7, 2015, 176 UD Officers have been hired in fiscal year 2015 and fiscal year 2016. The net gain from the influx of these 176 additional personnel has been 28 additional officers assigned to the White House. This represents a staffing increase of 4.8% at the White House Branch. At this time, we anticipate hiring approximately 288 total officers in fiscal year 2016.

Although Uniformed Division personnel assigned to the White House Branch has increased since the Protective Mission Panel report was issued on December 15, 2014, the overall number of personnel assigned to the Uniformed Division has decreased from 1,345 to the current number of 1,323, as of December 7, 2015.

With respect to the Protective Mission Panel recommendation to increase the Presidential Protective Division by 85 special agents, this will be complete in the 2nd quarter of fiscal year 2016.

Question 4. The Protective Mission Panel recommended an establishment of a leadership-development system to identify and train the agency's future managers and leaders. How do you identify the agency's future managers and leaders given that several of the agency's current managers and leaders have been investigated for misconduct?

Answer. When there is an open position in the Senior Executive Service (SES) ranks, the Secret Service Executive Resources Board (ERB) reviews the list of employees who have received SES certification from the Office of Personnel Management.

If an SES-certified employee is identified as being a viable candidate to fill the vacancy, the ERB makes a recommendation to the director for his consideration. If no current SES-certified employee is identified as being a viable candidate to fill the vacancy, the ERB makes a recommendation to the director to announce the vacancy to external candidates.

For non-SES supervisory positions, special agent career progression guidelines were established in September 2015, and a career track for non-law enforcement personnel is currently under development.

Question 5. As outlined in the latest Federal Employee Viewpoint Survey, the Department of Homeland Security is still struggling in areas of morale and leadership. The Secret Service in particular has been plagued with retention issues. Please describe what plan you have in place to address retention and ensure the Service is recruiting top, diverse talent?

Answer. A retention incentive program has been implemented for the Uniformed Division. Under the plan, officers signed retention bonus agreements in the amount of 5% of their annual salary and began receiving that bonus, in part, every 90 days they remained on the job. To date, over 90% of the eligible Uniformed Division members have executed a service agreement and are participating in this program. In addition, a comprehensive review of recruitment and retention flexibilities available within the Federal Government is currently being conducted.

The Talent and Employee Acquisition Management Division has developed and implemented a fiscal year 2016 Recruitment and Outreach Plan. The Plan outlines strategies that will guide the recruitment activities necessary to ensure the Secret Service recruits a highly qualified and diverse workforce that is representative of America. The plan includes traditional outreach, such as attending National and diversity-focused career fairs, information sessions and career fairs at Historically Black Colleges and Universities, Hispanic-serving institutions, and Tribal colleges and universities, liaison with military Transition Assistance Program/Army Career Alumni Program (TAP/ACAP) events, and attending National diversity conferences. In addition, new opportunities in social media recruiting are being leveraged to attract today's engaged candidates on LinkedIn, YouTube, Twitter, and internet radio providers such as Pandora and iHeartRadio. The strength of these platforms is their ability to target potential applicants with the backgrounds and skill sets we seek.

The Entry Level Assessment Center (ELAC) will continue to be used to process large groups of Special Agent and Uniformed Division Officer applicants through the hiring process. Typically during an ELAC, the applicant is administered 2 or more assessments of the hiring process in a reduced amount of time. During fiscal year 2016, 6 UD ELACs have been conducted with more than 460 applicants being processed to date.

The Recruitment and Outreach Plan is a living document and will be updated and revised as necessary throughout the fiscal year to meet the agency's goals in recruitment and hiring.

Question 6. It has been often stated that it is very difficult to transition from the Uniformed Division to the President's Protected Division. What percentage of agents in fact transfer from the Uniform Division to the Protected Division? What special programs are in place to support such a desire to transfer?

Answer. Uniformed Division officers do not ever transfer directly to a special agent position in the Presidential Protective Division, a permanent protective detail. In fact, no one applying for a law enforcement position within the Secret Service is hired directly to a position with a permanent protective detail. There is a period during which the expertise, maturity, and judgment essential to the extremely critical and demanding work of special agents protecting our Nation's highest elected leaders is developed in field offices supporting protective operations and conducting counterfeit currency, financial, or cyber crime investigations as criminal investigators.

Uniformed Division officers do frequently go through the necessary process to become special agents. Those Uniformed Division officers who become special agents are required to go back to the Federal Law Enforcement Training Center (FLETC) in Glynco, Georgia for the Criminal Investigator Training Program course. After graduation from FLETC they return to the U.S. Secret Service James J. Rowley Training Center (JJRTC) to attend the Special Agent Training Course. Upon successful graduation from the JJRTC the new agent is then assigned to a field office for the first phase of their career. After their initial field office assignment the agent is then transferred to a permanent protective detail, like the Presidential Protective Division or Protective Intelligence Division.

Question 7. In June of this year, it was reported that several dozen USSS Uniform Division Officers were placed on duty at the White House without completing the requisite security clearance process. In fact, over the last 5 years, approximately 643 officers and agents have been assigned to positions without the requisite security clearance. Please provide the demographical information to include race and gender for each officer and agent assigned to duty without a security clearance over the last 5 years.

Answer. A report is being compiled and will follow.

Question 8. Are agents and officers presently required to have a completed security clearance before being placed on duty? Please provide the number of agents and officers currently on duty without a security clearance, the specific post each agent or officer was assigned, the date of the assignment, and the length of time the agent or officer remained at this position without a clearance.

Answer. There are no agents or officers currently on duty without a security clearance. Pursuant to Secret Service policy, SCD–02(01), DHS has authorized the Secret Service to hire employees "contingent upon completion of a full-scope background investigation." Employees may be hired under this contingency if the Secret Service has completed the majority of a Single Scope Background Investigation (SSBI) and no derogatory information was developed which could adversely impact the candidate's ability to hold a Top Secret security clearance during the course of the SSBI. Employees hired under this contingency status are required to sign an SSF 4024, Conditional Access to Sensitive but Unclassified Information Non-Disclosure Agreement, prior to reporting for duty.

Question 9. In your testimony, you reference 14 contractors added to Secret Service staff to help adjudicate security clearances. What is the current average amount of time required by your staff to complete a security clearance since the addition of the contractors?

Answer. In an effort to correct the record, it should be noted that the statement in the testimony does not accurately reflect the number of contractors added to Secret Service staff to help adjudicate security clearances. The Security Clearances Division (SCD) is in the process of on-boarding 24 contractors to assist in the security clearance process. At this time, 11 are on board. The purpose of the contractors is to process the high volume of applicants to the agency to ensure adjudication before the personnel become operational while staying within the 114-day Office of the Director of National Intelligence (ODNI) standard.

Question 10. The Inspector General's memorandum on the improper database access states that there was evidence of only 1 individual out of 18 executive-level managers who attempted to inform the Director or higher levels of the supervisory chain about the information or attempt to remediate the activity. Do you find it concerning that some of your senior leadership, which you personally appointed, did not see error in this behavior?

Answer. The DHS OIG investigation found that 18 supervisors at the GS–15 or Senior Executive Service level may have known about improper database access but only one attempted to inform the director or higher levels of the supervisory chain about the information or attempt to remediate the activity. Additional investigation conducted by the Secret Service Inspection Division, with the authorization of the DHS OIG, included interviews of these supervisors which had not previously been conducted by the DHS OIG. This supplemental investigation revealed that other supervisors with knowledge of Secret Service employees improperly accessing databases or sharing protected information ordered their employees to immediately cease and desist accessing the database. Further, the vast majority of supervisors did not receive information that was attributable to a USSS data system, nor did they have any awareness that the rumor originated through potential misconduct.

Regardless, as I stated in testimony before Congress, I am committed to ensuring that all employees are held to the highest standards of professional conduct, whether on or off duty. I believe the behavior of the employees who violated existing Secret Service and DHS policies pertaining to the unauthorized access and disclosure of information protected by the Privacy Act of 1974 is unacceptable. I also believe that supervisors who failed to advise employees to cease and desist or attempt to inform higher levels of the supervisory chain after obtaining actionable information are also culpable. Those we protect and the public we serve expect us to live by our oaths and the values we have established as an agency, and we should demand nothing less from each other. We are better than the actions illustrated in this report and people, responsible supervisors and line employees alike, will be held accountable for their actions.

Question 11. Director Clancy, according to your testimony, when you heard of Representative Chaffetz's application for the Secret Service being discussed, you dismissed it as a rumor. However, according to the OIG's memorandum, you discussed this rumor at a luncheon with former directors of the Secret Service. Instead of investigating, you spread the rumor. What does that say about the culture of professionalism of the Secret Service?

Answer. I would like to address my statements and the decision of the OIG to reopen the investigation on October 5, 2015. During the process of reviewing the draft, I was reminded by a colleague that I had been informed of a rumor regarding the individual's application history on March 25. While I myself do not recall hearing of this rumor, several others have confirmed that I did, and that it was a general rumor about the individual's past application; it did not relate to USSS employees improperly accessing databases or sharing protected information. In order to ensure accuracy within the report, on my own initiative I contacted the OIG to correct the record. I made this decision because I feel that it is important to be as forthcoming, accurate, and complete as possible. I expect this from my employees and expect nothing less from myself.

The OIG published an addendum in October reporting its assessment of the updated information pertaining to when I was made aware of this rumor. Interviews with former directors, my deputy director, and my former chief of staff only serve to corroborate that the information available to me at the time was nothing more than a rumor. The information was not attributed to a Secret Service data system or indicative of any action—inappropriate or otherwise—by any Secret Service employee. Nothing in the addendum contradicts what I have maintained from the beginning—that at no time prior to April 2 was I aware that this rumor originated in information obtained through potential misconduct. When I did learn of it, I took immediate action, contacting the OIG and sending an official message to the workforce on the handling of sensitive information.

Question 12. According to the Inspector General's memorandum, the personal file from the data leak was stored on the Secret Service Master Central Index or MCI system. MCI is described as a "1980s vintage, electronic database and system of records." The National Security Agency conducted an analysis of the Secret Service data system in 2010. NSA concluded that the system was dated and fully operational only 60 percent of the time. Why was the system not updated or removed until July of this year, only after this particular data leak?

Answer. The MCI upgrade was part of the Secret Service's broader effort to modernize its IT systems. This effort, known as the Information Integration and Technology Transformation ("IITT") program, was established in fiscal year 2010. In recognition of the limitations of MCI and other mainframe applications, the Secret Service initiated the Mainframe Application Refactoring ("MAR") project in 2011 to assess the existing 48 applications residing on the mainframe and migrate necessary capabilities and accompanying data to a non-mainframe, secure, highly-available and compartmentalized environment. DHS estimated the project would take 10 years to complete. The Secret Service accelerated the MAR project in 2013 and was able to achieve project closure on June 24, 2015.

Question 13. What plans do you have in place regarding the MCI and other outdated systems within the Secret Service? What parameters are available to ensure such a gross mismanagement of access and authority does not occur again?

Answer. On March 24, 2015, there were technological security deficiencies within the Secret Service's primary internal database that contributed to the unauthorized access of information. These internal vulnerabilities have been addressed and the potential for similar misconduct in the future mitigated. The MCI was a mainframe application developed in 1984 that served as a central searching application and case management system. More specifically, MCI contained records from protective, investigative, and human capital divisions and served as a single access point for investigators and administrators. A significant deficiency of this arrangement was that an MCI user had access to all of the data in MCI regardless of whether it was necessary for that user's job function.

The Secret Service's Information Integration and Technology Transformation ("IITT") program was established in fiscal year 2010. In recognition of the limitations of MCI and other mainframe applications, the Secret Service initiated the Mainframe Application Refactoring ("MAR") project in 2011 to assess the existing 48 applications residing on the mainframe and migrate necessary capabilities and accompanying data to a non-mainframe, secure, highly available and compartmentalized environment. DHS estimated the project would take 10 years to complete. The Secret Service accelerated the MAR project in 2013 and was able to achieve project closure on June 24, 2015. At that time, all employee mainframe access was revoked. The new systems are completely operational, and all legacy data has been migrated to new platforms where data is locked down and access to data is dependent upon job function. Protective, investigative, and human capital records reside in different systems, and internal controls have now been implemented to restrict access to those systems in two ways. Now access is: (1) Limited to the respective directorates responsible for the information; and/or (2) based on the role of the system user within the organization. Shutdown of MCI began at the end of July, and it was fully powered down on August 12, 2015. Disassembly of the mainframe began in August 2015, and it was physically removed from the data center on September 16, 2015.

Question 14. In the past, you have placed agents and officers on administrative leave, suspended security clearances, and provided limitations on technology when agents are under investigation. Please explain your decision to not take immediate disciplinary action on the senior-level management and the other personnel who were identified as improperly accessing the MCI database.

Answer. Disciplinary action is taken only after investigation into the facts and circumstances is complete. In conjunction with this incident, the DHS OIG completed its investigation in later September and provided the supporting documentation in early October. In this instance, the agency did not have all of the information necessary from the OIG to contemplate disciplinary action until October 7, 2015. Even after receiving the information, in some cases, it was determined further investigation by our Office of Professional Responsibility was required.

Question 15. In your testimony, you state that the likely maximum disciplinary action each employee involved in the data breach will face is 12 days suspension. Does the table of penalties address violations of conduct that are also violations of law? Was there a discussion within the Office of Integrity and/or the Department of Homeland Security to revoke each individual's security clearance? If not, please explain why.

Answer. The Table of Penalties does contain penalties that are applicable for violations of law. The revocation of security clearances is handled by the Security Clearance Division rather than the Office of Integrity. Accordingly, there were no discussions within the Office of Integrity or between the Office of Integrity and the Department of Homeland Security regarding the revocation of security clearances.

Question 16. The improper database access issue seems to be an issue with integrity, which means doing the right thing, even when no one is looking. Please describe what trainings and communications are provided to Service employees promoting integrity. Please also describe how senior management promotes integrity to the workforce.

Answer. All senior executives, most Headquarters-based managers and supervisors, and all field office and protective division special agents in charge (SAICs) are required to receive ethics training every year. Training includes the use of non-public information.

LEG provides in-person training to all Washington, DC-based employees required to receive it (except when exigent circumstances warrant written training). SAICs outside the Washington, DC, area are required to participate in the Headquarters training sessions by video—or teleconference. LEG also visits the field offices and protective divisions in one domestic region each year to personally train the SAICs and all available supervisors. SAICs are encouraged to invite other available employees.

With respect to ethics training, in calendar year 2014, the Office of Chief Counsel (LEG) provided ethics training to 100% of those employees required to receive it. In calendar year 2015, LEG targeted a goal of 100% compliance and provided in-person training to a total of 587 employees. LEG reports the results of its training efforts annually to the Office of Government Ethics.

LEG oversees the publication and issuance of "Standards of Ethical, Professional, and Personal Conduct: A Desk Reference for United States Secret Service Employees." The desk reference is a comprehensive summary of the statutes, regulations, and policies that govern employee conduct. When the desk reference was first published in 2013, every employee was issued a printed, bound copy of the book. Subsequently, at the initial ethics briefing of the biweekly new employee orientation, LEG has provided new employees with a printout of the guide and referred them to the electronic version available on the Secret Service Intranet.

Additionally, during the winter of 2012–2013, an instructor-led course was developed entitled "Standards of Conduct (Ethics)." In 2013, this course was incorporated into many new recruit and in-service courses as depicted in the table below:

Basic Courses
- The basic course instructional blocks were entitled Ethical Decision Making & Standards of Conduct
  - Special Agent Training Course.—2.5 hours
  - Uniformed Division Training Course.—2.5 hours
  - Mixed Basic Training Course.—3 hours
  - Protective Detail Training Course.—3 hours
  - Counter Assault Team Basic School.—2 hours
  - Counter Assault Team Cycle Training.—2 hours

In-Service Courses
- The in-service course instructional blocks were entitled Standards of Conduct
  - 4th Shift Training.—2 hours
  - Firearms Instructor Training Course.—2 hours
  - Seminar for First-Line Supervisors.—45 minutes
  - SA Reintegration Course.—1.5 hours
  - UD In-Service Training Course.—1 hour

In addition to instructor-led training, there are also mandatory on-line ethics courses available to all employees through the Learning Management System (LMS). In April 2012, it became mandatory that all employees traveling overseas to take the on-line course entitled "Making Decisions Ethically." In March 2015, this course was replaced with the on-line ethics course entitled "Decision Making Elements," which became a mandatory, annual requirement for all USSS employees.

Question 17. The Secret Service has now replaced the MCI system and 95% of employees who once had access to the particular database in question no longer have access. Of the employees who will continue to have access, how many were implicated in this data breach? Please explain your decision to allow these individuals to continue to have access to sensitive information.

Answer. As discussed in the response to question 13, the MCI system was fully shut down in August of 2015. All legacy data was migrated to new platforms where data is locked down and access to data is dependent upon job function. None of the individuals identified in the DHS OIG investigation into the improper access and distribution of information contained within a Secret Service database now have access to applicant data information.

QUESTIONS FROM CHAIRMAN RON JOHNSON FOR JOSEPH P. CLANCY

Question 1. Inappropriate use of information systems is likely a security violation. What is the status of any on-going security clearance investigations and adjudications?

Answer. For the employees who were identified by the Department of Homeland Security (DHS) Office of Inspector General (OIG) as being involved in accessing a record containing personally identifiable information (PII) in the internal database, security clearance warning letters are being issued for inappropriate use of information systems.

Question 2. What is the reasoning for the Secret Service maintaining records of unsuccessful applications for an extended period of time that contain sensitive PII?

Does the Secret Service currently maintain similar records of unsuccessful applications that are not deemed relevant?

Answer. At the time of the events in question, the Secret Service was still governed by records retention schedules requiring this type of information be retained for 20 years. Due to the fact that these schedules were vetted, approved, and signed by the National Archives and Records Administration (NARA), adherence to these schedules was a matter of legal compliance. New NARA-approved retention schedules have now replaced the legacy schedules, and information relating to applicants who are not hired is held only for 2 years, unless a formal background investigation is conducted. If a formal background investigation is conducted, the case file is held for 5 years.

Question 3. Please describe the process to verify that Secret Service employees have reviewed the Secret Service Ethics Guide on an annual basis.

Answer. This guide was distributed electronically and in hard copy in 2013 in response to one of the Professionalism Reinforcement Working Group (PRWG) recommendations, which reads as follows:

"PRWG Recommendation.—Reinforcement of Ethical Behaviors: The USSS notifies its workforce regarding policy changes on discipline, including expectations on ethical behavior and conduct through issuance of policy directives. However, the USSS should use multiple approaches to reinforce the importance of ethical behavior and conduct at all times. For example, the USSS should consider issuing all current employees and all new employees a user-friendly, easy-to-read manual highlighting the organization's core values, compliance principles, standards of conduct, and the expectation that employees adhere to standards of ethical conduct."

The ethics guide provides a comprehensive summary of relevant statutes, regulations, and policies. Many of the rules in the ethics guide are contained in Secret Service manual sections to which employees certify on an annual basis via SSF 3218.

QUESTIONS FROM CHAIRMAN JAMES LANKFORD FOR JOSEPH P. CLANCY

Question 1a. During your testimony you were asked if the Secret Service maintains paper files with personally identifiable information (PII) in addition to the PII stored on electronic databases.

Does the Secret Service still maintain paper files in any of its offices containing personally identifiable information (PII)?

Answer. Yes.

Question 1b. If so, who has access to such files and how are those files stored?

Answer. Access to records containing such information is generally controlled by the access procedures set out under the Privacy Act of 1974, title 5 of the United States Code, section 552a (Privacy Act). System of Record Notices (SORNs) required under the Privacy Act which implicate record systems maintained by the Secret Service are published by the Department of Homeland Security (DHS), the Office of Personnel Management, and the Equal Employment Opportunity Commission. The SORN sets forth the routine uses for access to each system as well as the storage requirements for each system. Copies of Secret Service SORNs as most recently published by DHS are attached.

Question 1c. If so, what security controls does the Secret Service have in place to prevent, detect, and respond to the unauthorized access of any paper files containing PII in any of its offices?

Answer. Most types of PII records have specific additional regulatory storage, handling, and reporting protocols (e.g., storing in a locked room with access controls/logs). Information put into inactive storage includes a specific notation on National Archives form SF 135 that the files must be protected under the Privacy Act.

Question 2. In the context of Secret Service employee removal authority, you testified that you would like greater ability to dismiss employees that violate agency policy and the law.

What additional removal authority would assist you in changing the current culture and ensure that agency policy and the law is respected?

Answer. While we believe that current law allows for a reasonable process and means to remove employees from Federal employment in misconduct cases, the pace of that removal action is often slow and does not always foster a culture of accountability. For instance, when a case has been referred to, and accepted by, the OIG for investigation, the Secret Service can be delayed in taking action to address instances of employee misconduct, including criminal misconduct. In these instances the Secret Service must wait for the OIG to fully complete their investigation and issue a report which may lack the underlying evidence, sworn statements, and sometimes be in a redacted format. We believe that, if OIG were to provide the Secret Service with real-time information concerning evidence developed during an OIG investigation, we would, in some cases, be able to take expeditious disciplinary action against employees. For instance, if the OIG provided the Secret Service with a sworn statement in which the employee admits to the misconduct, the Secret Service could propose disciplinary action in advance of a receiving a finalized, formal report. In this regard, we will engage with OIG to explore this possible change to existing procedure and any other changes that may lead to a greater culture of accountability in the Service workforce.

Question 3. Concerning the topic of agency whistleblowers, you stated "everyone in the Service knows that whistleblowers perform a vital function" and "there's no retaliation" against them.

Can you explain the steps the Service is currently taking to ensure that all whistleblowers are properly protected and shielded from retaliation?

Answer. The Secret Service recognizes its obligation to protect the rights afforded to employees in making protected disclosures, including disclosures made to Congress, and values the benefits derived from the resulting oversight.

The Secret Service is committed to creating open lines of communication within the agency to ensure concerns raised at any level receive the attention they deserve, and to ensure that employees who bring concerns to light are praised for doing so, rather than retaliated against.

Biennial training on certain Federal anti-discrimination and "whistleblower" protections is required by the No FEAR Act for all Department of Homeland Security (DHS) employees. This No FEAR Act course was developed by the DHS Office for Civil Rights and Civil Liberties' (CRCL) Equal Employment Opportunity and Diversity Division and its CRCL Institute based on an anti-harassment training course created by the Central Intelligence Agency's Office for Equal Employment Opportunity Office.

Further, an agency-wide message was issued on October 30, 2015, regarding "Whistleblower Protection Awareness" which referenced policy manual sections related to disclosures to Congress and included a link to "information to help employees easily determine what they should report, how to report suspected issues, what training DHS offers, [and] what legal protections are available . . . ".

Additionally, Secret Service Manual guidelines requiring employees to report misconduct or retaliation were reiterated to all employees in an official message to the workforce on March 23, 2015. It is important that employees recognize the agency's position on this issue, and Director Clancy will continue to emphasize it to the workforce. The Secret Service fully respects and supports the rights of whistleblowers, and retaliation of any kind is not and will not be tolerated. These rights and protections are clearly stated in the Secret Service Ethics Guide, the Table of Penalties, and within the Secret Service Manual.

Question 4a. Your testimony outlined that recent Secret Service policy now requires the purging of applicant files every 2 years to improve internal protections of personally identifiable information (PII) housed on its databases.

When did this policy change?

Answer. This policy changed on October 1, 2015. Please note, at the time of the events in question, the Secret Service was still governed by records retention schedules requiring this type of information be retained for 20 years. Due to the fact that these schedules were vetted, approved, and signed by NARA, adherence to these schedules was a matter of legal compliance. New NARA-approved retention schedules have now replaced the legacy schedules, and information relating to applicants who are not hired is held only for 2 years, unless a formal background investigation is conducted. If a formal background investigation is conducted, the case file is held for 5 years.

Question 4b. What additional policies and training does the Secret Service have in place to ensure PII housed on its databases is not improperly accessed?

Answer. A Secret Service Information Resources Management (IRM) directive entitled "IRM Privacy Act Review" includes policy for reviewing new IT systems or changes to existing IT systems to determine Privacy Act impact. Related Secret Service and Department of Homeland Security (DHS) directives help ensure awareness of and compliance with PII regulations, through mechanisms such as the Privacy Threshold Analysis/Privacy Impact Analysis processes.

Existing policies and training include longstanding guidance regarding the proper access to databases and handling of Privacy Act protected information, which is clearly stated in the Secret Service Ethics Guide, in the Table of Penalties, and within the Secret Service Manual sections related to rules of behavior with respect to the use of information technology. Employees are required to certify annually that they have reviewed these manual sections.

Additionally, the Secret Service provides a 1-hour briefing to Special Agent and Uniformed Division Training Classes that includes material on the Privacy Act. A senior Government Information Specialist from the Freedom of Information Act and Privacy Act Branch of the Office of Government and Public Affairs teaches the class and focuses, in part, on PII.

A 1-hour in-service on-line training titled "IT Security Awareness" is required as part of the agency's Federal Information Security Management Act ("FISMA") obligations. The course outlines the role of Federal employees in the protection of information and in ensuring the secure operation of Federal information systems.

The Privacy Act is also discussed during in-service ethics classes administered to the field by Secret Service Office of Chief Counsel instructors.

Further, DHS requires Secret Service employees to complete annual in-service on-line training titled, "Privacy at DHS: Protecting Personal Information." This training was incorporated into the required curriculum in 2012 and covers proper handling of PII.

Finally, in August, the agency began including a dedicated block of instruction for the new Special Agent Training Classes regarding the Release of Information. The class provides an overview of the Privacy Act and the Freedom of Information Act, reviews employees' responsibilities under those Acts and the consequences for failing to fulfill them, and more generally, discusses the proper release and use of information employees have access to. A similar block of instruction for the Uniformed Division Training Classes was added in November. Further, additional training is provided to new hires at Secret Service New Employee Orientation.

Question 4c. Has the Secret Service implemented any additional policies and training in response to recent improper and illegal accesses?

Answer. In light of the DHS OIG report of September 25, 2015, and subsequent addendum of October 22, 2015, specific guidelines have been established and are effective for processing disciplinary and adverse actions resulting from the misuse of Secret Service database systems and/or the unauthorized disclosure of sensitive information. Additionally, and as stated above, in August, the agency began including a dedicated block of instruction for the new Special Agent Training Classes regarding the Release of Information. The class provides an overview of the Privacy Act and the Freedom of Information Act, reviews employees' responsibilities under those Acts and the consequences for failing to fulfill them, and more generally, discusses the proper release and use of information employees have access to. A similar block of instruction for the Uniformed Division Training Classes was added in November. Further, additional training is provided to new hires at Secret Service New Employee Orientation.

QUESTIONS FROM CHAIRMAN SCOTT PERRY FOR JOHN ROTH

Question 1a. After you issued the management alert on the Chaffetz PII incident, Director Clancy contacted your office in order to revise his recollection of events. This in turn caused you to reopen the investigation and issue an addendum to the original report.

Has this ever occurred in any of your other reviews?

Answer. No.

Question 1b. Based on the conclusions in your addendum, would you be comfortable updating the original conclusion in your report that indicated Director Clancy was not aware of the improper PII access until April 1? If so, when would you say Director Clancy became aware of the incident?

Answer. The addendum serves as an update to the original report, and concludes that on March 25, Director Clancy learned from at least 3 separate sources that Chairman Chaffetz may have applied to the Secret Service. We are unable to conclude, because Director Clancy has no memory of it, the degree to which he understood how widely the information was being disseminated through the Secret Service, or whether he understood that the discussion was being fueled and confirmed by dozens of agents improperly accessing Secret Service data systems.

Question 1c. Do you have concerns that Director Clancy provided a false statement to your investigators when originally interviewed?

Answer. The earlier statement was inaccurate in that he originally stated that he was "fairly certain" that he first learned of it on April 1, the day before the media reports. We do not have any evidence as to his state of mind at the time he made the statement.

Question 2a. On the OIG website, you list management alerts, which are designed to "inform senior DHS managers of conditions which pose an immediate and serious threat of waste, fraud, and abuse in agency programs." Since July 2014, of the 5 of the 15 management alerts have involved the Secret Service. This is concerning given that the Service is significantly smaller than other DHS components.

How do the USSS misconduct statistics compare to other agencies within the Department?

Question 2b. In your opinion, and experience, do the Secret Service misconduct statistics compare to other agencies of comparable size across the Federal Government? Is it average, above average, below average?

Answer. We have not done a statistical comparison of misconduct allegations and cases between Secret Service and other DHS components or other agencies in the Federal Government. Certainly the allegations involving the Secret Service that have come to light since the 2012 events in Cartagena, Colombia are of grave concern and our reviews over the past several years point to on-going organizational and management challenges. During the current fiscal year, we will continue our oversight of the Secret Service, including a review of its implementation of the recommendations of the Protective Mission Panel. In addition, we intend to evaluate the strength of the Department's disciplinary processes. We will focus this review on the depth and breadth of employees' perceptions and attitudes about misconduct and the application of discipline, DHS's established rules of conduct, and the application of discipline across the Department.

QUESTIONS FROM RANKING MEMBER BENNIE G. THOMPSON FOR JOHN ROTH

Question 1. Since the Protective Mission Panel, you have had to be involved in investigating the Secret Service for personnel misconduct. You have also issued two management advisories for the agency in 2015. Based on your investigations of the Secret Service, what is the agency lacking? What does it need to change?

Answer. The Secret Service needs to understand the requirements for building an ethical culture within their organization, which consists of three elements: (1) Leaders (not just the top leader, but all through the organization) who create a "tone at the top" and demonstrate their commitment to an ethical culture by both words and deed; (2) a commitment to both the words and the spirit of a meaningful code of conduct; and (3) creating a system of accountability for all of those in the organization—leaders and the rank and file—who deviate from that.

I believe that the Secret Service needs improvement in all three areas. That the leadership has not created the appropriate tone is apparent from the significant number of senior leaders and managers who did nothing once they found out about the conduct. We also had the deputy director of the Secret Service who failed to provide information during his initial interview. This sends the message to the rank and file that such behavior, notwithstanding a written code of conduct, is acceptable. While we are satisfied that the Secret Service has taken steps since the Cartagena incident to establish a more uniform discipline system, I believe that more could be done to ensure that deviations from the code of conduct are addressed.

Additionally, for an organization to change—and I believe that the Secret Service is in great need of change—the individuals within the organization must understand that there is a need for change, and individuals must be empowered to create that change. I do not see within the upper levels of the organization such an understanding. Typically, in those circumstances change does not occur until there is a disruptive external event that forces the organization to change.

78

Question 2. Your office issues management alerts to senior leadership of DHS when your office finds conditions that pose a serious concern. You have issued management advisories for the Secret Service in April 2015 and in October 2015. Your October 2015 management advisory actually warns that protectees could be in immediate danger if changes are not made. Looking at the Secret Service overall, what does it say about the agency to have two management advisories issued in such a short period of time?

Answer. Both management alerts were ultimately caused by Secret Service's inability to execute basic management functions in support of its mission. The April 2015 alert was the result of not replacing an alarm system at a Presidential residence that had been installed in 1993. We found that the Secret Service did not have a formal system to report and track security technical problems, maintenance and repair needs, and upgrades. Likewise, we found that the staffing shortages that we believe led to the officer fatigue issues were caused by the lack of a staffing and hiring plan that first would understand the number of personnel needed to staff the White House Complex without a reliance on excessive overtime, and second, would ensure the necessary administrative infrastructure to be able to efficiently hire to the proper level.

Question 3. In October, you released a management alert after 2 agents were observed asleep on the job. You cited long overtime hours and fatigue as a reason for your concern. The Secret Service publicly stated it does not agree with your findings. Please describe how you reached your conclusion and what caused your observations to rise to the level of an alert.

Answer. The management alert occurred after we observed agents asleep during 2 different site visits, at different locations, weeks apart, on July 15 and August 11. As auditors are trained to do, we looked to see if there may be a root cause for this. We found that the overtime for 1 officer for the previous 8 weeks amounted to 157 hours—an average of being required to work 60 hours per week for 8 straight weeks. The second officer's overtime totaled 73 hours for the previous 6 weeks, for an average of 52 hours per week.

We also found that overtime among the Uniform Division has substantially increased in the last few years. In fiscal year 2013, it averaged 362 hours per position; in fiscal year 2015, it averaged 597.4 hours per position—a 39% increase in 3 years. We also found that the problem was getting worse, not better. The overtime was necessary because of a lack of officers; yet, in fiscal year 2015 the Uniform Division lost 162 officers through attrition, but managed to hire only 152—a net loss of 10 officers. Finally, we found that until recently the Secret Service had not engaged in a staffing plan or model to understand the staffing level it would need to ensure that it did not rely on excessive overtime to accomplish its mission.

Question 4. Does the Management Alert issued by your office indicate any connection between these incidents and either absent or ineffective Secret Service policies to ensure sustainable staffing practices and work-life balance?

Answer. Yes. As I indicated in the answer to the last question, the Uniform Division officers are being asked to take on an unsustainable burden. What concerned us is the lack of effective response from the Secret Service leadership. The Protective Mission Panel alerted the Department to this a year ago, and yet, as evidenced by the failure to hire even to the current level of attrition, the Secret Service has not responded in a manner that recognizes the severity of the problem. Hence, the management alert.

Question 5. Improving morale at DHS is of particular priority to this committee and myself. You state in the management alert that USSS reported that "it recognizes that employee morale suffers when decreased staffing levels result in increased overtime and travel requirements, and decreased opportunities for training." In your time investigating the Secret Service, have you observed times where morale is in fact impacted? What factors would you say contribute to low morale in the Service?

Answer. There is significantly low morale within the Secret Service. As noted in the most recent results of the Federal Employee Viewpoint Survey, the Secret Service is second to last. We believe that the inability to address the fundamental management issues, including outdated technology and insufficient staffing, is a significant driver of poor morale.

Question 6. Based on your investigation, were personnel within the Service sufficiently informed of the proper use of USSS computer systems and the care needed for sensitive information, whether via training, manuals, oral communications, etc.?

Answer. Yes. Secret Service policies include Information Technology Rules of General Behavior that cover employees' use of all Secret Service IT systems. The policy requires employees to safeguard Sensitive, Classified, and privacy-related information against unauthorized disclosure to the public. It further requires that all Secret

Service personnel acknowledge review and understanding of the provisions enumerated in that policy upon entering on duty with the Secret Service and annually thereafter. In addition, the Secret Service's Table of Penalties includes penalties for unauthorized use of a Government computer and disclosure of information in violation of the Privacy Act.

Also applicable to the Secret Service are DHS-wide policies contained in the *DHS Handbook for Safeguarding Sensitive Personally Identifiable Information,* which also prohibits all employees from browsing files containing Sensitive PII out of curiosity or for personal reasons.

In addition to these policies, the log-on screen for the MCI database contained specific warnings that the system could be used for authorized Government business only.

Question 7. You state in your memorandum that although agents were trained on use of the system and received yearly refresher trainings, it was apparent that many of the agents disregarded that training. What did you observe in your investigation that led you to this conclusion?

Answer. In response to interview questions by OIG agents, many of the Secret Service employees who authorized Chairman Chaffetz' MCI record without authorization insisted that their actions were appropriate. Some acknowledged ignoring the warning banner on the MCI logon screen. Others thought that accessing the database, even without a legitimate business purpose, was okay because it was "our database."

Question 8. Your office only reviewed the MCI system for those individuals who accessed Congressman Chaffetz' personal file. Therefore, it is possible that other individuals were also searched in the database. Based on your review of the system and interviews with Service employees, do you believe employees frequently utilized the MCI system improperly, in particular to research individuals? If so, how frequently do you believe this occurs?

Answer. Based on our interviews, it appeared that there was a casual attitude about the rules regarding the use of the system. This was obvious in the number of individuals who conducted improper searches of Chairman Chaffetz' name. We found no reason that this did not occur before for other individuals.

Question 9. Based on your experience in accountability and law enforcement across the Federal Government, do you have any concerns about these employees' status while under adjudication? As DHS Inspector General, would you advise Department and Secret Service leadership to change policies related to employees subject to disciplinary review in any way?

Answer. The use of paid administrative leave for DHS employees facing misconduct investigations and adjudications is a matter currently being reviewed by the Government Accountability Office and we look forward to reviewing the analysis and recommendations contained in its upcoming report.

We should note that as a general matter, Federal law allows agencies to suspend an employee indefinitely without pay if there is reasonable cause to believe that a crime has been committed for which a term of imprisonment may be imposed. Laws and policies regarding employees subject to disciplinary review should ultimately be balanced against critical due process safeguards to ensure fairness and consistency to the Federal workforce.

QUESTIONS FROM CHAIRMAN JAMES LANKFORD FOR JOHN ROTH

Question 1a. During your testimony you indicated that the MCI database was unable to audit accesses without a specific program written for each search term.

Since the migration to an updated database system, what audit capability and checks (automatic or manual) are now in place?

Answer. We are currently conducting a technical security assessment of the Secret Service's updated database systems that when complete, will answer this question. Specifically, our Office of Information Technology Audits is reviewing the information systems the Secret Service currently uses to store and retrieve data and information previously stored in the MCI database. Our assessment is designed: (1) To verify that the MCI is in fact no longer in use, (2) identify which systems currently house MCI data, (3) determine the level of physical and system controls implemented to secure the data from further instances of unauthorized access, and (4) identify gaps in the security posture. We plan to issue our final report in February 2016, and I look forward to discussing our conclusions with you and your staff at that time.

Question 1b. Based on your investigation, would a regularly occurring, agency-wide OIG audit of PII searches help change Secret Service culture regarding the protection of PII?

Answer. We believe that the best way to prevent future activity of the type we saw here would be for Secret Service to focus to a greater degree on its information security program. Modern data systems with appropriate audit and access controls, when coupled with appropriate agency processes, policies, and procedures, would prevent unauthorized access to information. Every year, we audit, pursuant to the Federal Information Security Act (FISMA), DHS' information systems. FISMA requires IGs to perform evaluations of Departmental implementation of the 11 program-level security authorization activities. DHS OIG performs tests to determine how the Department's components are implementing these activities.

From fiscal year 2013 to the present, Secret Service has done poorly on these FISMA reviews compared with other DHS components. For example, as of September 2015, USSS failed to meet the Department's "security authorizations" target of 100% for "high value assets" and 95% for "all other FISMA systems" as USSS only scored 75% and 58% respectively. In addition, USSS only scored 38% in "weakness remediation," where the Department's target was 90%.

We believe that focusing on modernizing and securing Secret Service data systems, in combination with training and other efforts to create an ethical culture (such as a uniformly administered system for dealing with deviations from a defined standard of conduct) are the best way to change the culture with regard to the use of PII.

Question 1c. Based on your investigation, what recommendations would you make to change Secret Service culture regarding PII?

Answer. As noted in the above question, the systems that the Secret Service uses to store PII must have audit and access controls that help ensure the security and confidentially of Privacy Act-protected records. Training about PII and its appropriate handling and safeguarding should be reinforced and reemphasized. Ultimately, change will come when management does not tolerate the deliberate or grossly negligent mishandling of PII and employees who violate Department and Secret Service policies and/or the Privacy Act face disciplinary consequences for their actions.

Question 2a. Your testimony reflects that agents seemed to consider personal data on Secret Service databases as theirs to access as they pleased.

What training policy updates have been or should be made to correct this mindset reflected in your investigation?

Answer. Our investigation did not determine what changes, if any, Secret Service has made to their training policies as a result of this incident. Our next FISMA audit will determine the overall level of training Secret Service personnel receive.

Question 3a. The September 2015 Department of Homeland Security (DHS) Office of the Inspector General (OIG) report titled "Investigation into the Improper Access and Distribution of Information Contained Within a Secret Service Data System" did not audit the 45 Secret Service employees for unauthorized access of personally identifiable information on the agency's databases prior to the Congressman Chaffetz matter starting on March 25, 2015.

Should DHS OIG conduct additional audits of these 45 Secret Service employees for unauthorized accesses prior to this date?

Answer. We share the concern that it is possible that these specific employees mishandled or accessed files without authorization prior to this specific investigation—whether related to Chairman Chaffetz or others. Due to the technical limitations of the MCI database, it would be nearly impossible for us to conduct additional audits of these 45 employees. Moreover, according to the Secret Service, the MCI mainframe has been disassembled as of September 2015 so it is unclear whether additional audits can be performed on the system.

QUESTION FROM CHAIRMAN RON JOHNSON FOR JOHN ROTH

Question. The DHS OIG concluded that 4 of the 45 Secret Service employees that accessed the PII information of Congressman Chaffetz were authorized to do so. What was the criterion for determining if the Secret Service employee that accessed the information of Congressman Chaffetz in the MCI database was authorized or unauthorized?

Answer. To determine whether Secret Service employees were authorized or unauthorized to access Chairman Chaffetz' information in the MCI database, we analyzed whether they had an official purpose to access the record. Officials who examined the record in connection with the performance of assigned duties and who had to access the record in order to perform those assigned duties properly were considered authorized.

For example, employees at a specific field office received a press inquiry as to whether Chairman Chaffetz had applied to that office. While the office appropriately declined to comment to the press, as part of their due diligence, they accessed the system to determine whether it was true. Likewise, one employee in headquarters was directed by his superior to do so, as part of deciding what management steps to take.

However, a number of supervisors accessed the information, purportedly to determine whether the talk about Chairman Chaffetz was true. Accessing the record in that circumstance was inappropriate and not in connection with an official purpose because the truth or falsity of the information was irrelevant to directing their subordinates to use Secret Service data systems only for official Government purposes, and not to satisfy personal curiosity. This was especially the case since, with a few narrow exceptions, these supervisors did nothing with this information, such as reporting it up the chain to their superiors.

QUESTION FROM CHAIRMAN SCOTT PERRY FOR JOEL C. WILLEMSSEN

Question. Based on your expertise and what you have heard today, how can agencies, and specifically DHS and the Secret Service, ensure they have the proper internal security controls so that only the right employees, with a need to know, can access sensitive information such as PII?

Answer. Agencies first need to establish and communicate policies for collecting, storing, accessing, using, and retaining personally identifiable information (PII)[1] and other sensitive information. The policies should state when it is appropriate to access such information, when it is not, and the consequences for willful noncompliance. In addition, managers, supervisors, and employees should be informed and trained regarding their respective responsibilities for safeguarding PII.

In addition, agencies, including the Department of Homeland Security (DHS) and the Secret Service, can implement several protective measures to control access to PII and other sensitive information. As we reported in September 2015,[2] access controls limit, prevent, or detect inappropriate access to computer resources, including PII and other sensitive information, thereby protecting them from unauthorized use, modification, disclosure, and loss. These controls include ensuring that only personnel with a need to know are authorized access to sensitive information. Agencies implement authorization controls by, for example, uniquely identifying all users, periodically reviewing system access, disabling accounts of users who no longer need access, and assigning the lowest level of permission necessary for a task.

Agencies should also implement audit and monitoring controls, which establish individual accountability, monitor compliance with security policies, and investigate security violations. These controls help determine what, when, and by whom specific actions have been taken on a system and can be used to monitor users' access of sensitive information, including PII. To implement controls for monitoring access, agencies can install software that provides an audit trail or logs of system activity that can be used to determine the source of an action or activity.

QUESTIONS FROM RANKING MEMBER BENNIE G. THOMPSON FOR JOEL C. WILLEMSSEN

Question 1. GAO's September 2015 report on information security speaks directly to weaknesses in limiting, preventing, and detecting inappropriate access to computer resources. Please provide us with examples of what other Federal agencies are doing to better monitor inappropriate internal data access.

Answer. As we reported,[3] agencies can monitor inappropriate data access by implementing audit and monitoring controls. These controls establish individual accountability, monitor compliance with security policies, and investigate security violations. Audit and monitoring controls help determine what, when, and by whom specific actions have been taken on a system and can be used to monitor users' access to sensitive information such as PII. In March 2015, we reported[4] that the Internal Revenue Service (IRS) continued to enhance its audit and monitoring capability. Specifically, IRS had strengthened the audit and monitoring processes of its

---

[1] PII is any information that can be used to distinguish or trace an individual's identity, such as name, date and place of birth, Social Security number, or other types of personal information that can be linked to an individual, such as medical, educational, financial, and employment information.

[2] GAO, *Federal Information Security: Agencies Need to Correct Weaknesses and Fully Implement Security Programs,* GAO–15–714 (Washington, DC: Sept. 29, 2015).

[3] GAO–15–714.

[4] GAO, *Information Security: IRS Needs to Continue to Improve Controls over Financial and Taxpayer Data,* GAO–15–337 (Washington, DC: Mar. 19, 2015).

mainframe by enabling the monitoring of changes to certain controls over the management of data.

In addition, the Treasury Inspector General for Tax Administration (TIGTA) monitors access and refers instances of willful unauthorized inspection of taxpayer data for administrative actions or prosecution. For example, according to TIGTA, for fiscal years 2014 and 2015, its Office of Investigations successfully prosecuted 15 investigations. Seven of the 15 were for violating the Taxpayer Browsing Protection Act of 1997.[5] The remaining 8 were prosecuted for unauthorized access related to the use of a Government computer.

Question 2. Your September 2015 report lists 5 different areas of potential weaknesses in agency compliance: Did GAO's analysis find weaknesses in compliance by DHS in any of these 5 areas, and if so, which one(s)?

Answer. Yes, our analysis of agency, inspector general, and our reports identified weaknesses at DHS for all 5 areas. These areas included controls intended to: (1) Limit unauthorized access to agency systems and information; (2) ensure that software and hardware are authorized, updated, monitored, and securely configured; (3) appropriately divide duties so that no single person can control all aspects of a computer-related operation; (4) establish plans for continuing information system operations in the event of a disaster, and (5) provide a security management framework for understanding risks and ensuring that controls are selected, implemented, and operating as intended.

Question 3. Earlier this year, GAO released a report stating that OMB, in consultation with DHS, should enhance its security program reporting guidance and located information security weaknesses. Speak to your findings as it relates to this particular data leak. What improvements should DHS, and in particular the Secret Service, implement in areas of access control, segregation of duties, and security management?

Answer. Our findings do not specifically address the incident that occurred at the Secret Service. However, the Federal Information Security Modernization Act of 2014 (FISMA)[6] now requires OMB to include in its annual report to Congress a summary of major agency information security incidents, such as the incident at the Secret Service.

In September 2015, we reported[7] on the adequacy of the information security policies and practices of the 24 agencies covered by the Chief Financial Officers (CFO) Act of 1990.[8] Like most other agencies, DHS had weaknesses in each of the 5 control areas we track, including access controls, segregation of duties, and security management.

To improve their access controls, DHS and the Secret Service should ensure the enforcement of the principle of "least privilege," where employees are granted the minimum level of access necessary to perform their duties. DHS and the Secret Service should also ensure that incompatible duties are separated and that employees understand their responsibilities. Separation of duties can be implemented through formal operating procedures, supervision, and reviewing access authorizations, among other things.

To improve security management activities, both DHS and the Secret Service should ensure that they fully implement entity-wide information security programs so that risks are understood and that effective controls are selected, implemented, and operating as intended.

Question 4. Can you confirm that given the scope of GAO's engagement, analysts collected information with regard to information-security compliance by the Department of Homeland Security overall, and did not collect any information with regard to Secret Service practices specifically?

---

[5] The Taxpayer Browsing Protection Act was enacted on August 5, 1997, and made willful unauthorized inspection of taxpayer data illegal. Pub. L. 105–35, 111 Stat. 1104 (1997).

[6] The Federal Information Security Modernization Act of 2014 was enacted as Pub. L. No. 113–283 (Dec. 18, 2014). FISMA 2014 largely supersedes the very similar Federal Information Security Management Act of 2002 (FISMA 2002), Pub. L. No. 107–347, Title III (Dec. 17, 2002), and expands the role and responsibilities of the Department of Homeland Security, but retains many of the requirements for Federal agencies' information security programs previously set by the 2002 law.

[7] GAO–15–714.

[8] The 24 Chief Financial Officers Act agencies are the Departments of Agriculture, Commerce, Defense, Education, Energy, Health and Human Services, Homeland Security, Housing and Urban Development, the Interior, Justice, Labor, State, Transportation, the Treasury, and Veterans Affairs; the Environmental Protection Agency; General Services Administration; National Aeronautics and Space Administration; National Science Foundation; Nuclear Regulatory Commission; Office of Personnel Management; Small Business Administration; Social Security Administration; and the U.S. Agency for International Development.

Answer. As part of our audit of Federal agencies' implementation of the provisions of FISMA, we collected information on the information security efforts of the 24 Federal agencies covered by the CFO Act, including DHS. However, we did not collect or receive any information regarding specific security practices at the Secret Service.

Question 5. Does it seem reasonable to you to conclude that Secret Service faces some of the management challenges highlighted in the latest High-Risk Update, and that leaders of the Secret Service must demonstrate the "continued perseverance" in improving agency management culture that the Comptroller General calls for in the Update?

Answer. Yes, it would be reasonable to conclude that the Secret Service faces some of the same management challenges. For example, in the most recent update to our High-Risk series [9] we lauded DHS's progress in strengthening its management functions, but concluded that the Department still faces significant management challenges. Such challenges include improving employee morale, a challenge that the Secret Service could also face with its employees.

For example, according to the Partnership for Public Service's 2015 rankings of the Best Places to Work in the Federal Government, the Secret Service ranked 319 of 320 agency subcomponents Government-wide. Additionally, according the Partnership for Public Service's analysis of Federal Employee Viewpoint Survey data, employee satisfaction and commitment among Secret Service employees consistently declined from fiscal year 2011 through fiscal year 2015.

Question 6. In your testimony, you state that this particular improper data access is the most common among agencies—too many individuals having access to a broad range of data unrelated to their job responsibilities. What solutions are available to fix this broad information access and better monitor employees' use of data systems?

Answer. In September 2015, we reported [10] that 22 of the 24 CFO Act agencies had weaknesses with limiting, preventing, and detecting unauthorized access to agency systems and information. Specifically, 18 agencies had weaknesses in controls that are intended to limit user access to only that necessary for performing their work. When granting access to users, agencies should provide only the minimum access necessary for performing their duties. In addition, agencies should implement audit and monitoring controls to monitor users' access of sensitive information such as PII. These controls can help determine what, when, and by whom specific actions have been taken on a system.

QUESTIONS FROM CHAIRMAN JAMES LANKFORD FOR JOEL C. WILLEMSSEN

Question 1a. Your testimony reflects that the Social Security Agency has personal identifying information (PII) on nearly every U.S. citizen, and that agencies such as the VA, Department of Education, and CFPB also house substantial amounts of PII.

What are the most effective means for auditing employee access of PII at these agencies?

Answer. As we reported in September 2015,[11] agencies should use audit and monitoring controls to establish individual accountability, monitor compliance with security policies, and investigate security violations. These controls help determine what, when, and by whom specific actions have been taken on a system and can be used to monitor users' access of sensitive information, such as personally identifiable information (PII).[12]

To monitor users' access and actions, agencies can install software that provides an audit trail or logs of system activity that can be used to determine the source of an action or activity. Agencies can also monitor users' access by implementing other technologies such as network- and host-based intrusion detection systems, security event correlation tools, and computer forensics. Network-based intrusion detection systems capture or "sniff" and analyze network traffic in various parts of a network.

Question 1b. Which Government-wide, unimplemented GAO recommendations concerning PII protection should be put into place first?

Answer. We currently have 1 Government-wide PII-related recommendation whose implementation status we are evaluating. This recommendation was made to

---

[9] GAO, *High-Risk Series: An Update,* GAO–15–290 (Washington, DC: Feb. 11, 2015).

[10] GAO–15–714.

[11] GAO, *Federal Information Security: Agencies Need to Correct Weaknesses and Fully Implement Security Programs,* GAO–15–714 (Washington, DC: Sept. 29, 2015).

[12] PII is any information that can be used to distinguish or trace an individual's identity, such as name, date and place of birth, Social Security number, or other types of personal information that can be linked to an individual, such as medical, educational, financial, and employment information.

the Office of Management and Budget (OMB) in our 2013 report[13] regarding our finding that the 8 agencies we reviewed had inconsistently implemented data breach policies and procedures. We recommended that, to improve the consistency and effectiveness of Government-wide data breach response programs, OMB should update its guidance on Federal agencies' responses to PII-related data breaches. OMB neither agreed nor disagreed with our recommendation.

According to OMB, it has set a date of March 16, 2016, for updating its PII protection guidance to reflect current best practices and recent lessons learned regarding privacy protections and data breach standards.

Question 2a. You testified that it was perplexing to you why the Secret Service would still have PII information on Congressman Chaffetz from 2003, given the National Archives and Records Administration (NARA) requirement to properly dispose of such information once it is no longer needed.

How well are agencies complying with the NARA requirements to dispose or archive personal information once it is no longer needed?

Answer. We have not performed work specifically addressing the extent to which agencies are complying with the National Archives and Records Administration's (NARA) requirements for disposing or archiving personnel information that is no longer needed. However, in May 2015, we reported that Federal agencies took actions toward implementing requirements set forth in a NARA and OMB joint directive on managing Government records.[14] To illustrate:

- Twenty-three of the 24 Federal agencies we reviewed implemented the requirement to develop and begin implementing plans to manage all permanent records in an electronic format.
- Twenty-one of these 24 agencies implemented the requirement to identify for transfer and reporting those permanent records in existence for more than 30 years.
- Twenty of the 24 agencies implemented the requirement to identify all unscheduled records that have not been properly scheduled.[15]

Nevertheless, 5 agencies we reviewed did not fully meet those requirements, and we recommended that they and NARA take certain corrective actions. We did not make any recommendations to the Department of Homeland Security (DHS).

Question 3a. Under the Federal Information Security Modernization Act of 2014 (FISMA) the Office of Management and Budget (OMB) is required to maintain oversight responsibilities of Federal information security programs and ensure minimum security requirements for Government-wide information security programs and practices.

What is your assessment of OMB's fulfillment of these responsibilities over the last several years?

Answer. During the 12 years from when the Federal Information Security Management Act of 2002 (FISMA 2002) was enacted into law to when it was largely replaced by FISMA 2014,[16] Executive branch oversight of agency information security has evolved. As part of its FISMA 2002 oversight responsibilities, OMB issued annual instructions for agencies and inspectors general to meet FISMA 2002 reporting requirements. During that time we made recommendations to OMB for improving its oversight of agencies' security programs. For example, in 2013 we recommended[17] that OMB and DHS provide insight into agencies' security programs by developing additional metrics for key security areas such as those for periodically assessing risk and developing subordinate security plans. We also recommended that metrics for FISMA reporting be developed to allow inspectors general to report on the effectiveness of agencies' information security programs. OMB generally

---

[13] GAO, *Information Security: Agency Responses to Breaches of Personally Identifiable Information Need to Be More Consistent,* GAO–14–34 (Washington, DC: Dec. 9, 2013).

[14] GAO, *Information Management: Additional Actions Are Needed to Meet Requirements of the Managing Government Records Directive,* GAO–15–339 (Washington, DC: May 14, 2015).

[15] Scheduling is the means by which agencies identify Federal records, determine time frames for their disposition, and identify permanent records of historical value that are to be transferred to NARA for preservation and archiving. Unscheduled records are those records that have not had their value assessed or their disposition determined.

[16] The Federal Information Security Modernization Act of 2014 was enacted as Pub. L. No. 113–283 (Dec. 18, 2014). FISMA 2014 largely supersedes the very similar Federal Information Security Management Act of 2002 (FISMA 2002), Pub. L. No. 107–347, Title III (Dec. 17, 2002), and expands the role and responsibilities of the Department of Homeland Security, but retains many of the requirements for Federal agencies' information security programs previously set by the 2002 law.

[17] GAO, *Federal Information Security: Mixed Progress in Implementing Program Components; Improved Metrics Needed to Measure Effectiveness,* GAO–13–776 (Washington, DC: Sept. 26, 2013).

agreed with our recommendations. DHS also agreed with our recommendations and identified the actions it had taken or planned to take to address them.

In February 2013, we reported [18] that when OMB transferred several of its oversight responsibilities to DHS through a joint memorandum,[19] it was not clear how the two organizations would share these responsibilities. In that report, we suggested that Congress consider legislation to better define roles and responsibilities for implementing and overseeing Federal information security programs. In December 2014, Congress passed FISMA 2014 to improve cybersecurity and clarify cybersecurity oversight roles and responsibilities, among other things.

FISMA 2014 is intended to address the increasing sophistication of cybersecurity attacks, promote the use of automated security tools with the ability to continuously monitor and diagnose the security posture of Federal agencies, and provide for improved oversight of Federal agencies' information security programs. The act also clarifies and assigns additional responsibilities to OMB, DHS, and Federal Executive branch agencies.

In carrying out its FISMA responsibilities, OMB has increased its efforts to oversee agencies' implementation of information security. For example, OMB created the Cyber and National Security Team, called the E-Gov Cyber Unit, to strengthen Federal cybersecurity through targeted oversight and policy issuance. In September 2015, we reported that OMB, along with DHS, had increased oversight and assistance to Federal agencies in implementing and reporting on information security programs.[20]

In June 2015, in response to the Office of Personnel Management security breaches and to protect Federal systems from emerging threats, the Federal Chief Information Officer launched a 30-day Cybersecurity Sprint.[21] As part of this effort, the Federal Chief Information Officer instructed Federal agencies to immediately take a number of steps to further protect Federal information and assets and to improve the resilience of Federal networks.

Most recently, in October 2015, OMB issued a cybersecurity strategy implementation plan that is intended to strengthen Federal civilian agencies' cybersecurity.[22] The plan is to address Government-wide cybersecurity gaps through five objectives: (1) Prioritized identification and protection of high-value information and assets; (2) timely detection of and rapid response to cyber incidents; (3) rapid recovery from incidents when they occur and accelerated adoption of lessons learned from the Cybersecurity Sprint assessment; (4) recruitment and retention of the most highly-qualified cybersecurity workforce; and (5) efficient and effective acquisition and deployment of existing and emerging technology. The plan address our recommendation that the White House develop an overarching strategy for improving cybersecurity.[23]

Question 3b. What GAO findings regarding OMB's oversight of Government-wide information security programs demonstrate the greatest risks for exposure of PII?

Answer. As previously mentioned, we reported [24] that the 8 Federal agencies we reviewed generally developed, but inconsistently implemented, policies and procedures for responding to data breaches involving PII that addressed key practices specified by OMB and the National Institute of Standards and Technology. We attributed agencies' inconsistent implementation of data breach policies and procedures to incomplete guidance from OMB.

Also, in 2012, we reiterated [25] our previous finding reported in 2008 [26] that while the Privacy Act, the E-Government Act, and related OMB guidance set minimum

---

[18] GAO, *Cybersecurity: National Strategy, Roles, and Responsibilities Need to Be Better Defined and More Effectively Implemented*, GAO–13–187 (Washington, DC: Feb. 14, 2013).

[19] OMB, Memorandum M–10–28, *Clarifying Cybersecurity Responsibilities and Activities of the Executive Office of the President and the Department of Homeland Security* (Washington, DC: July 6, 2010).

[20] GAO–15–714.

[21] In June 2015, the Federal Chief Information Officer launched the 30-day Cybersecurity Sprint, during which agencies were to take immediate actions to combat cyber threats within 30 days. Actions included patching critical vulnerabilities, tightening policies and practices for privileged users, and accelerating the implementation of multi-factor authentication.

[22] OMB, Memorandum M–16–04, *Cybersecurity Strategy and Implementation Plan for the Federal Civilian Government* (Washington, DC: Oct 30, 2015).

[23] GAO, *Cybersecurity: National Strategy, Roles, and Responsibilities Need to Be Better-Defined and More Effectively Implemented*, GAO–13–187 (Washington, DC: Feb. 14, 2013).

[24] GAO–14–34.

[25] GAO, *Privacy: Federal Law Should Be Updated to Address Changing Technology Landscape*, GAO–12–961T (Washington, DC: July 31, 2012).

[26] GAO, *Privacy: Alternatives Exist for Enhancing Protection of Personally Identifiable Information*, GAO–08–536 (Washington, DC: May 19, 2008).

requirements for agencies, such laws and guidance may not consistently protect PII in all circumstances of its collection and use throughout the Federal Government and may not fully adhere to key privacy principles. We stressed that unilateral action by OMB might not be the best way to strike an appropriate balance between the Government's need to collect, process, and share personally identifiable information and the rights of individuals to know about such collections and be assured that they are only for limited purposes and uses. We suggested that Congress consider amending applicable laws such as the Privacy Act and E-Government Act by:

- revising the scope of the laws to cover all PII collected, used, and maintained by the Federal Government;
- setting requirements to ensure that the collection and use of personally identifiable information is limited to a stated purpose; and
- establishing additional mechanisms for informing the public about privacy protections by revising requirements for the structure and publication of public notices.

○

www.ingramcontent.com/pod-product-compliance
Lightning Source LLC
Chambersburg PA
CBHW081228280526
45787CB00006B/2570